TAKEDOWN

How an Undercover Cop Dismantled the Biggest Drug-Smuggling Ring in Maine

Allan T. Duffin and Darryl J. Kimball

published by

duffin creative

los angeles

Published in the USA by
Duffin Creative
11684 Ventura Blvd #205
Studio City, CA 91604
Visit us on the Web at duffincreative.com

ISBN-10: 0692504222
ISBN-13: 978-0692504222

First Edition
Printed in the United States of America

Table of Contents

Introduction

In March 1983, undercover detective John Arnold testified in federal court against drug dealer Richard Stratton. At the time, it was the biggest drug bust that the state of Maine had ever seen: $1.5 million (worth $3.6 million today) in hashish, marijuana, and cocaine. When the trial concluded, Stratton went to jail, and Arnold went back to his life as a small-town cop.

In the years since, Richard Stratton became a successful novelist and film producer, while John Arnold, who longed for a quiet life with his family, still works for law enforcement in a smaller role.

This is the story of how John Arnold, an unassuming police officer who stumbled onto the biggest case of his law enforcement career, brought a resourceful drug dealer to justice.

Chapter 1

THE FARM

Milton, New Hampshire, was—and still is—a town of fewer than five thousand people. Winters were wet and bone chilling, and passing storms sometimes piled snow as high as the tallest house. Snowplows often roared across town to keep the streets clear for traffic.

The Arnold family—Robert, Irene, and their sons John, Robert, and Richard—lived on a hundred-acre farm that was perched on the eastern border with Maine. Regular pursuits included hunting, fishing, and growing vegetables.

As a child, John Arnold cuddled under his blanket at night,

listening to the bitter wind howl through the trees outside. He learned early to be resourceful. When he was fourteen he would singlehandedly install snow chains on the tires of his father's old Ford truck.

John's father was a military veteran. After serving in the U.S. Army from 1939 to 1943, Robert Windel Arnold married Irene Cleta Coffman, a Texan. Robert was no stranger to big families, having grown up with twelve brothers and sisters. He was the youngest of the clan and would live until he was eighty-seven years old. Meanwhile, his wife Irene toiled in a local shoe factory to help support her family.

"I can't say that my father and I were really close," said John, "but we had a good family, and during Christmas we had all kinds of things. Neighbors' kids would give us presents. We always had birthday presents as well."

The couple's three sons weren't close either. John liked to hunt, while his older brothers Robert and Richard spent their time working on cars. When they were older, the three boys would move in separate directions, never growing closer.

Their father worked twelve to sixteen hours a day as an electrician in a Navy shipyard. He purchased the family farmhouse and land, and did all of the electrical work himself. He also installed equipment so that the house had running water, accessible from an old water pump on the kitchen counter that was connected to a rock well outside.

Live deer sometimes wandered around the property. From time to time the Arnolds hunted deer for food. "We'd also butcher cows," recalled John. "Sometimes we'd name the cows by months—one cow would be April and another would be May, for example—based on the month we were going to butcher them.

"We also raised cattle, cows, chickens, and pigs," John continued. "We had a wood-burning stove in the basement. I was generally the one who had to cut the wood and haul it down to the stove. We always had to do chores before fun. Mom canned a lot of beans, squash, string beans, and other vegetables from our big garden."

John wasn't much of a swimmer; he was "just a little afraid of the water." The pond on the family farm was deep enough for the water to reach just over the kids' heads. One summer, when John was about sixteen, his father dropped by the pond, where John and his two brothers were hanging out. Dad chatted a bit, noticed that John was the only one who wasn't swimming, and picked the boy up and chucked him into the pond.

"Now you need to learn to swim," said Dad.

John dog-paddled his way out of the pond and eventually learned how to swim. Eventually he rid himself of his fear and became a very good swimmer. "I didn't know it at the time," he recalled, "but this would come into play years later when I jumped into an ice-covered river and swam under the ice to rescue a drowning boy."

Mom Arnold made meals using all kinds of wild ingredients, and she baked delicious pies as well. She taught John how to cook, and it became one of his regular chores. He still has her old cookbook today, and cracks it open and uses it from time to time. John cooks the "old farm way—a little of this, a little of that," he explained.

"The only problem I have is that I'm used to making large portions for my family," said John. "By the time I'm done, I have a huge kettle and don't know what to do with all of it. When I cook, I overcook. I get that from my mother."

One day John's father decided to make hogs head cheese, a meat jelly made—as the name implies—from the head of a hog. "I came home one day and saw a big pot on the stove cooking," said John. "I picked up the cover, and to my surprise, there was a pig looking right at me!" His father was cooking it down to strip all of the meat.

A nearby creek, packed with fresh trout, was another source of food for the Arnold family. "I was standing underneath a bridge when the fish and game truck came along and restocked the creek," said John. "They dumped a whole load of trout over the side of the bridge, right in front of me. I didn't know if it was fishing season or if I was supposed to have a fishing license, but I was able to catch a whole passel of fish for the family that night."

To augment the family finances, John set up a vegetable stand near the road. The stand was unmanned, and customers paid on the honor system. "On a picnic table I set a can for customers to drop their cash into, and I spread out vegetables from our garden. 'Take what you want; pay what you want.' That was how we did it." Each day John came home from school and peered into the can to see how much money he'd made that day. Then he'd give the cash to his mother.

The Arnolds weren't middle class—"definitely a little on the poor side," remembered John. "Mind your elders and work hard," his parents told him, "and things will work out in the long run." Every year before school started, Mrs. Arnold took money she'd saved from working in the shoe factory to buy each of her children a new pair of dungarees. Since John was the youngest child, he received a lot of hand-me-down clothing.

Each morning John walked half a mile to the bus stop, where he'd catch the bus to school. Since there were only thirty-five students in his class, "everybody knew everybody," he said. John did well academically, making good grades. He was elected president of his class and voted Most Likely to Succeed. "I didn't read too much, but I loved math and science," said John.

At an athletic five-foot-nine and one hundred twenty-five pounds, John excelled at basketball. Because he had to stay late after school for basketball practice, John would walk all the way home—nearly ten miles—although sometimes he was able to hitchhike.

He received his first award at the New Hampshire state foul-shooting tournament, where he hit forty-nine of fifty shots from the foul line. "Every day during recess I was allowed to take a student with me and go to the gym and practice to get ready," he said.

During those days there were no drugs in the school. "I think we barely knew what drugs were," recalled John. "There was no pot either." It was the same for alcohol. John and his friends didn't try alcoholic beverages until their senior year in 1967. Even so, drinking was "not a big deal back then," he said.

When he was sixteen, John borrowed his mother's Volkswagen Beetle and drove the ten miles to downtown Middleton with several friends. One of them wanted to buy beer. "He knew that a VW has a good hiding spot for beer under the back seat," remembered John. After hiding the beer, the group headed back to the country. Once they got there, a state trooper pulled in behind them and motioned them to the shoulder. John steered the Volkswagen to a stop and took a deep breath. *I'm dead*, he thought.

The trooper ambled up to the driver's window and leaned in a bit, studying John's face.

"You got beer in this vehicle?" the trooper asked.

"No sir," John stammered.

"Uh-huh," said the trooper. "Mind if I search your vehicle?"

The trooper knew exactly where to look. As John recalled years later, "He went straight under the back seat and got the beer."

The trooper stared at John. "You are in violation for illegally transporting alcohol."

Rather than issue John a ticket, the trooper took the beer, stuck it in his patrol car, and drove away. John thought that was the end of it, so he never said anything to his parents.

What John didn't know was that his father was somewhat politically connected and knew people in the New Hampshire state government. One month later, John received a letter in the mail: the government was suspending his license for thirty days. "Now I was stuck," recalled John. "Do I tell my parents? I knew they were going to ask me to drive someplace at some point, but I didn't want to break the law and get in more trouble." Eventually John showed his father the letter.

"Son," said his father, "if you'd told me when it happened, I could have taken care of it. Next time something happens, good or bad, you come and see me. We can help."

John never forgot what his father had told him. "One of my biggest fears was getting into trouble with my father," John said. "I definitely learned my lesson with this one."

"Both of my parents were exceptional, in my mind," he said. "Later in life I would become very close to them. When I got older I left the nest, but years later I returned. Our bond grew deeper and deeper and greater and greater."

Chapter 2

OCEAN TIDE

AFTER HE GRADUATED from high school, John wasn't sure what he wanted to do. To keep busy, he worked for a time in the same shoe factory that his mother did. There weren't many jobs in the small community, so John appreciated whatever work he could find. He also continued working on his family's farm. "Dad used to say, 'Chores before play,'" recalled John. "Do your chores, and then you can go have fun. To us, 'play' was to go to the beach, or to take a walk."

John's father continued his day job as an electrician on nuclear submarines. Promoted up the civilian ranks, his father was offered an opportunity for higher pay if he'd work at shipyards in overseas locations. He chose to move to Guam.

Because he was still a student, John Arnold was allowed to accompany his parents on their trip. However, "just before the trip they decided to postpone it for a year," recalled John. His father wanted to wait until his next promotion came through. The bigger paycheck would be helpful.

By this time the other two Arnold brothers had moved out of the family home, leaving John alone with his parents. One day his father sat him down.

"John, you need to go to school, or do something," he told his son. "I'm sending you to a state teacher's college."

Tuition in the late 1960s was about $1,000 a semester—a lot of money in those days. John attended Plymouth State University, which was founded in 1871 as a teacher training school, for just a year and a half. "I didn't do a lot of studying," he said. "I wasn't a good student. I took music classes but failed them because I wasn't interested. I was getting by in English and math, but studying to be a teacher wasn't really what I wanted to do."

In January 1969 John's parents got a second chance to move overseas. "They knew I wasn't very happy at the school," said John, "so they asked if I wanted to go with them, and I jumped at the chance. I had nothing holding me back; I had no interest except in being alive. We all packed up our bags and left the farm behind with someone to take care of it."

John was just nineteen years old. He traveled to Guam by

airplane. He had never traveled outside of the United States, and he'd never been on an airplane.

Compared to the bitter New England winters, the weather in Guam was warm and beautiful. John stepped off the airplane into a sunshine paradise of palm trees, fruit growing everywhere, a deep blue ocean, and beaches of pure white sand. At the time the population was only about eighty thousand—half of what it is today. "There were twenty-six miles of roads around the whole island," recalled John. "The island was only thirty miles long and four and a half miles wide. It was a dream place for a kid."

On Guam was an American naval base and hospital. At the end of World War II the Japanese had left a lot of their equipment behind, including their heavy guns. John spent a lot of his free time wandering the island and studying war relics.

The local populace spoke a language called Chamorro, but they also spoke clear English. White Americans were known as "honkies," but they were welcome and encouraged to live there.

John's social life got a boost when his father shipped his car—a bright-red 1968 GTO convertible—to the island. The locals hadn't seen that style of automobile too often. "When I drove my father's car around," said John, "everyone would stop and look. You can imagine how many dates I had while driving that car!"

Chapter 3

BECOMING A COP

JOHN WAS TWO YEARS out of high school and didn't have much to do, but he was enjoying his time on Guam. His parents didn't want him to stagnate, and they urged him to find a job.

In February 1969, a month after arriving on the island, John took the civil service exam. He thought his score of 87 percent was low, but he was recommended for a position as a firefighter or police officer. Having watched police shows on TV for much of his childhood, John figured that being a police officer would be an interesting job. Nevertheless, he waited to see which department had an opening.

Soon he received a phone call from the police department. John was accepted as a probationary officer with an annual salary of $5,304 (about $33,800 today). The money wasn't an issue for him; he'd remain living in his parents' house for the time being.

At the age of twenty, John Arnold took his oath and was appointed to the position of public safety patrolman in the Guam Department of Public Safety (Police Division). It was March 23, 1969.

The academy didn't start for two months, so during the interim John went on ride-alongs with police officers and assisted at the police station. Since he was a white American "honky," the prisoners called him a lot of different names from behind bars. John didn't really know what his role at the station was except to call for help if something happened. He felt scared, sitting around for eight hours a day, watching prisoners and not really knowing what he was doing.

John's academy class had about twenty students in it, and he was one of two "honkies" in the class. The instructors taught in Guamanian but would review their subjects in English. John was able to pick up the Guamanian language fairly quickly. He found the academy pretty easy: he liked what he was doing, he found it interesting, and he enjoyed learning about firearms and the law. Since he was an expert shot from all of the hunting he'd done on the family farm, John enjoyed firing the police department's .357 Magnum revolver. He especially liked criminology: processing crime scenes and figuring out how and why a crime had occurred.

Although he'd always been a good athlete, John was one of the smaller men at the academy, and he struggled to keep up with the rest of his class during physical training. *It seems like a lot of people in the academy are in much better shape than I am*, he thought, *and much more agile*. Several of the Guamanian students could leap into the air, execute a flip, and land squarely on their feet. Since he was a small guy, John tried his best to hold his own. He learned how to talk himself out of situations rather than relying on physical brawn.

Academy studies included limited information about drugs and narcotics. The instructors showed the students what marijuana and cocaine looked like, but that was the extent of their drug training.

John enjoyed the real-world details for which the students could volunteer. When President Richard Nixon visited the island in the summer of 1969, John and several other academy students worked traffic control. Another volunteer assignment was doing guard duty, in pairs, at local bars. When a customer got too drunk or too rowdy, John and his partner would "hook the customer up" (put him in handcuffs), throw him in a police car, and take him to the station.

On one occasion John's partner was a Guamanian with a typical build: six feet tall and two hundred fifty pounds. If a fight broke out, John wasn't much help; he worked more as a backup to his partner since he'd never been in a bar fight. (In fact, until then, John had never been in a bar.)

During the last week of September 1969, with a week left until graduation from the police academy, John received a letter in the mail. It was an induction notice: he had been drafted into the U.S. Army on a lottery pick by the draft board in Dover, New Hampshire. He was told to be on an airplane bound for Fort Ord, California, on September 22.

John was furious. He visited the governor's office on Guam and requested an extension.

"I'm sorry, John," said the secretary. "You have no choice."

"But I'm scheduled to graduate from the police academy in a week!" said John.

The administrator shook her head. "You have to be on that plane to Ford Ord, or you'll face criminal action. I'm sorry."

John stomped out of the governor's office. He couldn't understand why the army couldn't wait a week so he could complete the police academy. He talked to everyone he could think of, including his parents, who couldn't help either.

A two-year stint in the U.S. Army seemed like forever. At the time, many inductees were fleeing to Canada to avoid the draft, but John wasn't that kind of person. He had to come to terms with what was happening. He'd never liked being told what to do, and he sure didn't like the government telling him what to do.

On September 22, John climbed the air stairs into a camouflage-colored military aircraft and sunk into a seat. He felt disgruntled. He didn't want to go—not only because he hadn't completed the police academy but also because he was leaving a lot of friends behind.

At twenty years of age, he thought he had a lot of things going on, and they were more important than the army.

Years later, looking back, John would feel that the army probably did a favor in drafting him.

Chapter 4

MILITARY POLICEMAN

ON SEPTEMBER 22, 1969, John Arnold was twenty years old and scared—a draftee on an airplane full of volunteers and draftees. He was headed to boot camp at Ford Ord, California.

"When I arrived at boot camp, I got the lesson of my life," John said. "First there were the medical physicals. Then they shaved our heads, gave us uniforms, and put us in open barracks to live. I learned pretty quickly that you didn't talk back to the drill sergeant. I can't remember how many times I was kicked or thrown to the ground to do push-ups because I asked the wrong question or hadn't done something correctly.

"Throughout boot camp I learned very quickly after so many times of being beaten up and thrown on the ground, that the government had all the rights and I had none," he noted.

One positive thing about the six-week boot camp was that John improved himself physically. He learned hand-to-hand combat, and he learned how to box. "I don't remember being beat up so much in my entire life," John recalled. He scrambled under a wire course under machine-gun fire, stumbled through a house where trainees yanked their gas masks off to experience what tear gas felt like, and practiced shooting with the M16 rifle. He threw hand grenades and fired .45 Colt automatic pistols, qualifying at the expert level.

On November 22, 1969, John successfully completed boot camp and traveled to the army's military police school at Fort Gordon near Augusta, Georgia, where he would receive technical training for the next four months. Since he'd received law enforcement training on Guam and his aptitude test supported it, the army felt he'd be a natural fit as an MP.

At MP school John learned about military and civilian regulations, the UCMJ (Uniform Code of Military Justice, the "lawbook" for the military), traffic laws and rules, arrests and restraints, and how to conduct an investigation. Most of the courses were easy to get through, since John had already received police training on Guam.

Four months passed quickly, and in February 1970, John received new orders: he was to report to Fort Benjamin Harrison near Indianapolis, Indiana. This would be his first real law enforcement job "working the street."

John's squad had eight MPs, all of whom lived in a barracks. They worked the night shift and reported to the provost marshal (the "chief of police" on the installation). "It was very close to today's police work," recalled John, "but on a small scale. We worked within the jurisdiction of the base. There were also a lot of civilians who came and went on the base each day, as well as quite a number of bars and clubs in the area."

The squad patrolled the post in Willys jeeps that had canvas tops. Normally two MPs rode in each jeep. Occasionally they transported prisoners in the back. The squad investigated accidents, enforced speed limits, and did crime prevention. Most of the MPs in John's squad were eighteen or nineteen years old and held the rank of private first class. Because of his prior academy experience, John was given a Spec 4 (Specialist 4) rating—just beneath a sergeant. He was a year or two older than the rest of the guys.

Routine patrol could be quite boring, and sometimes the squad hunted for something to keep it busy. "We kept hearing about a colonel on base who was a drunk, and that he pretty much drove everywhere drunk," said John. "We were told to leave him alone because he was a colonel. But you have to keep in mind, even in my twenties I was a very stubborn, persistent, straightforward person, and now the government had put me in a place I didn't want to be. I was just not going to let a colonel or any other rank break the law or the rules of the base."

One night John and his partner were on patrol in their jeep and were discussing the drunk colonel. In the darkness they saw another jeep rumbling down the wrong side of the road. The MPs stopped the car. The colonel in question was behind the wheel.

In those days there was no field sobriety test, but John was sure he had the colonel for drunk driving. "He had been all over the road," said John. "When I stopped him, he stumbled out of the jeep and fell on the ground. His eyes were bloodshot. Everything was there. It was an easy case for me to prove."

The following day, the provost marshal summoned John and his partner.

"Leave the colonel alone," said the provost marshal.

John was confused. "I'm sorry, sir?"

The provost marshal leaned over his desk. "You are not to arrest him again. Understand?"

"But—"

"Leave him alone, Arnold."

John and his partner left the building. "You can imagine how pissed off I was," John recalled. "First, I was drafted into this man's army. Didn't want to be there, but there I was. I had no family nearby, and now I am told to look away and not do my job."

John told the rest of the squad what had happened. "We came to an agreement that if we saw this same vehicle—the colonel's jeep—and he was drunk, we were going to arrest him no matter what."

During the next two weeks, John set up on military bars and clubs in the area, watching for any sign of the colonel's jeep. It was nowhere to be found.

Not long afterward, John and his partner were on patrol and received a radio call to respond to an accident. When they arrived at the scene, they saw a jeep with its front end smashed into a telephone pole. Behind the wheel was the colonel, drunk as a skunk.

John arrested the colonel on a drunk-driving charge for the second time. The MPs towed the damaged jeep away and filed their paperwork. "We were all happy that that we had busted the colonel again," said John, "and we were waiting for the scolding that we knew would be coming from the provost marshal."

A week went by, and there was no word from the provost marshal. John's squad was pretty happy. "We thought we had won," he recalled. "However, we started getting the feeling that something was brewing. We weren't quite sure what it was. We knew the court case would be several months down the road, and I knew I would have plenty of time to prepare for my case in court."

Two weeks passed. The MPs got a call to report to the provost marshal's office. All eight soldiers and their supervisor arrived on time. The provost marshal stood up and handed each of them travel orders. They were being reassigned. John looked down at his travel orders and peered at the destination.

Vietnam.

"I told you to leave this colonel alone," said the provost marshal. "Now you are all being transferred to Vietnam."

The MPs looked at each other, speechless. "At the time we didn't think it was such a big deal," said John. "Then we realized that, by transferring all of us to Vietnam, there would be no one to testify in court against the colonel, and his case would be dismissed. How convenient was that?"

Chapter 5

VIETNAM

"At the time, I was still a little bit of a wise-ass," John recalled. "I didn't really care. So what? They were going to send me to Vietnam. I only had a year and a half left on my orders at this point. So off to Vietnam it was."

On July 18, 1970, John arrived at Long Binh Post, the gigantic U.S. Army installation near Saigon. He carried a full G.I. backpack and duffel bag with his clothes packed tightly inside. At the supply depot he was issued an M16 rifle, ammunition, a Colt .45 pistol, and an M79 grenade launcher.

During his yearlong deployment, John was attached to Company C of the 720th Battalion, 18th Military Police Brigade. Company C was part of the military police unit that protected convoys running north on the back roads toward Da Nang. During each patrol in his V-100 armored reconnaissance vehicle, John manned the .50-caliber machine gun that was mounted on the back. He quickly learned how to shoot, tear down (disassemble), and repair the weapon.

During his first five months in Vietnam performing convoy escort, John and the rest of the crew lived in their V-100. On a regular mission, they would leave Long Binh, geared up with C-rations, and travel with the convoy to its destination. "Sometimes it would be several hundred miles," John recalled. "Some trips would be nice, easy trips, but some would involve gun battles on the way. We lost some people and some jeeps during this time."

John remembers sleeping and eating in the V-100, sometimes for two weeks at a time. Whenever they returned to Long Binh, the MP crew had six or seven days of downtime while a different squad went out to escort the convoys.

John wasn't in country long before he saw his first dead body. A bloated Vietnamese woman's corpse lay on the road along a convoy route. "We weren't sure how she had been killed," said John, "but it was obvious she had been there for three or four days. It was a scene that left an impression on me."

Then there were the firefights in the jungle. American troops called the North Vietnamese Army and Viet Cong soldiers "gooks." Generally the enemy wore all-black clothing. "They would open up on us, trying to stop the convoy," said John. "Bullets came in on our position—these were the tracer rounds fired by the enemy."

Because American tracers were red, John could tell who was firing and where the rounds were coming from. "Every sixth or seventh enemy round was green. You'd see them coming toward you, and they would disappear before reaching you." By contrast, American M16 rifles fired red tracers every third or seventh round.

Many American soldiers choose not to talk about the battles they fought during wartime, and John is no exception. "I've seemed to black out much of what happened during the firefights...the specifics of them, anyway."

During one convoy mission John was asked to drive the V-100 armored vehicle. He thought it would be good to do something different, and driving the V-100 was similar to driving a truck.

"But then we got ourselves in the middle of a big firefight, and the captain started shouting orders at me about what to do and where to drive," said John. "I guess I just froze up and panicked. I was used to being the gunner. The captain was shouting for me to turn around and backtrack, but I turned off the road and stopped right there."

John's squad survived that battle without taking on casualties, but his driving days were over: he was back on the .50-caliber gun, and that's where he stayed. "I guess it was for the better," he mused. "After that firefight, I knew I would rather shoot than steer."

The periodic firefights during convoy missions gradually took their toll. John was scared, shaken up, and started to worry if he'd make it back home alive at the end of his tour. Patrol duty kept him busy, but John still wanted to go home and be a cop.

As John recalled, "I was a twenty-year-old kid with an M16 rifle, a .45-caliber pistol strapped to my hip, and all the hand grenades I could carry, manning a .50-caliber machine gun on the back of an armored vehicle. It should have been the time of my life, but I didn't want to be there. I just had to endure it until I could get myself out the jungle and back to doing police work somewhere."

After six months riding through the jungle, John transferred to Saigon and was attached to the U.S. Army Criminal Investigation Division, or CID. He wore civilian clothes and investigated crimes in which military personnel were involved. Some of the cases involved drugs. At the time, John didn't understand how so many G.I.s could be on drugs, but later he realized that they took drugs in order to survive the harsh realities of the war.

John and other CID personnel traveled the streets of Saigon and bought drugs from "mama-sans" and "papa-sans." "I recall many times having a paper bag full of vials of heroin that we would buy from the mama-sans," said John. "Often they would try to run, and we would grab them." On many cases the CID personnel worked with the Vietnamese police.

During some investigations John flew by helicopter to military bases around the country. "The bases looked just like the ones you see in the movies," he recalled, "with the sandbags, barbed-wire perimeters, bunkers, and everything." The trips were often for narcotics investigations, but there were other types of crimes as well.

In one case, a soldier rolled a grenade under his captain's bunk, killing the captain. John was flown in by helicopter to assist in the murder investigation. As the helicopter hovered over the base, John thought to himself, *Hell, I'm only twenty-one years old, and here I am, working on a murder investigation!*

Although John's social life had slowed considerably since he'd left Guam, he still found time to hit the nightclubs in Saigon. "The smell of Saigon always seemed to linger in your nose," he said, "particularly the local food." He ate well, and he enjoyed the cuisine.

One day John's CID supervisor, a staff sergeant, came to him and barked, "John, you need to be on this plane to the Philippines to see your parents."

John was confused. "Are my parents okay?" he asked.

"Yes," said the sergeant. "Now grab your bag and go!"

Soon John was headed to the P.I. [Philippine Islands] for a little R&R—military parlance for "rest and relaxation," a mental break from the war zone. "I thought that something bad had happened," he said, "but it was nothing more than my parents wanting to see me. I realized that my dad had some political clout among the higher-ups somewhere."

John was helicoptered to an aircraft carrier off the coast, and then found himself strapped into a small jet aircraft as it roared off the deck, en route to Clark Air Base in the Philippines.

Officer John Arnold, c. 1972. Photo by Lt. Norman Paul
of the Sanford Police Department.
JOHN ARNOLD COLLECTION

Chapter 6

BACK TO SAIGON

JOHN ENJOYED VISITING his parents in the Philippines. He was only scheduled for a week's stay, but a typhoon rolled in and he had to stay another week.

Then he was back in Saigon, picking up where he'd left off, taking down Vietnamese drug suppliers with the assistance of the local police.

Finally, John's one-year tour of duty was over. He'd survived his time in country and was happy to leave it behind him.

On his way home John was sent through Hawaii to Oakland

Army Base in San Francisco Bay, where he went through debriefing, which was required of everyone coming back from the war. Eventually he reached Pease Air Force Base in Portsmouth, New Hampshire—his final stop. It was late August of 1971. He was almost home.

But when John's airplane landed, he was shocked at what he saw.

"I wasn't able to wear my uniform because people were pointing fingers and yelling," he said. "While we were on the plane, we were told not to tell anyone where we were coming from, and not to say that we had been to Vietnam. So that's exactly what I did. I kept quiet. I was shouted at; I was ridiculed. It really surprised me because I did not even want to go to war. But the mere fact that I had been there was enough for some people. It was a pretty bad experience."

He flew to Boston and then Portsmouth, New Hampshire. There was no one at the airport to meet him. His parents were still overseas and his two brothers were at home, tending to the farm. John threw his backpack over his shoulder, strolled over to a main road, and stuck his thumb out at the passing traffic. He hitchhiked from Portsmouth back to his home in Milton—about 140 miles.

John walked into his family's house and hung up his uniform. (To this day he keeps his army dress uniform in his closet. On the green Class-A jacket are his National Defense Service Medal, Vietnam Service Medal, Campaign Medal, and Good Conduct Medal.)

Soon his parents returned home to Milton, and the family was together again. John looked for a new job. Unfortunately there were few available, so he went to the unemployment office and applied for unemployment compensation, drawing on it for several months until he landed a job as a security officer. During every shift he walked inside a warehouse and checked doors to ensure they were secure.

One day John saw an advertisement for a job opening at the police department in Sanford, Maine, about ten miles away. *Hey, maybe I can finally be a cop, like I wanted*, he thought.

John applied for the job by mail. While he waited to hear back from Sanford, John purchased his first car, a 1968 Chevy Chevelle—"all white, my dream car," he recalled. He also looked up his old high school classmates—it had been four years since they had graduated—but most of them had left town.

John loved his car. One day he was driving through Rochester, a city south of Milton, and heard his stomach rumble. He swung into a Dairy Queen, strolled up to the counter, and ordered some fried clams.

Behind the counter was "the most beautiful blonde girl I had ever seen," he said. "She burned my clams, and then she apologized."

Her name was Peggy Beach, and it was love at first sight.

As the old saying goes, "When you know, you know." The couple had dated for just one month when John asked Peggy to marry him. He was twenty-two years old when they tied the knot on February 22, 1972, and they are still married today.

The year 1972 was good for the newlyweds. John received a job offer from the Sanford police department just one week after the wedding.

The Sanford police department was aware of John's military and law enforcement background, and sent a Capt. Roy and Sgt. Cote to the Arnold home to interview John. They wanted to know if John was interested in working undercover, purchasing drugs on the streets of Sanford. Since John would be new in town, no one would recognize him.

John agreed. He and Peggy packed up and moved to Sanford, Maine, a small town of twenty thousand people about ten miles from the Atlantic Ocean and near the New Hampshire border. The local industry was composed mainly of factories and mills. Since there were no high schools within the city limits, all of the students were bused to county schools elsewhere.

The police department was located in the town hall, an old brick building with an underground garage. Across the street was a Dunkin' Donuts, where all of the police officers got their coffee each day. Although local shops are sometimes known to be generous to law enforcement officers, "the coffee was never free," John recalled with a grin.

The tiny department was supervised by Chief John Pride, a deputy chief, a captain of patrol, and a captain of detectives. Each of the three daily shifts had eight personnel in total: six officers led by a sergeant and a corporal. However, "we generally had somebody on vacation," recalled John, "so we were lucky to have five or six patrol people per shift."

When the administrative and command staffs went home at

5:00 p.m. each day, town security was the responsibility of the shift supervisor. "I remember the first time I was the duty patrol sergeant," said John. "I sat there thinking, *Wow! I'm the primary person responsible for security in the entire city of Sanford!* Later, the department sent John to the Maine Criminal Justice Academy to get his state certification as a law enforcement officer.

The mills in Sanford used water from the Mousam River, which ran through the middle of the town. Runoff from the river formed several large ponds, one of which, known as Number 1 Pond, was ten acres in size and situated in the downtown district. Number 1 was a popular place for ice skating during the winter months.

During their off-hours, many millworkers frequented the several nightclubs in town. One of those places was called the Wolf Club, which hosted fights among its patrons every Friday and Saturday evening. The bar fights got so large that the police usually responded with multiple units.

Sanford also had a pool hall, a hospital, two department stores (Ames and Woolworth's), and a McDonald's, which was the only fast food restaurant in the city. The Washington Square Restaurant was a stone's throw from the police department and would become important to John in the near future.

It would be a while before John could wear his uniform on duty. During his first two months in the police department he walked the streets buying drugs from different dealers. "I was mostly purchasing marijuana and LSD and mickeys," he said, "which were stamp-like stickers with blots of ink on them. The LSD was on the stamp."

John Arnold as a corporal in the Sanford
Police Department, mid-1970s.
Photo by Harrison of the *York County
Journal Tribune.*
JOHN ARNOLD COLLECTION

Chapter 7

FIRST TIME UNDERCOVER

WHEN JOHN PERFORMED undercover work during his first several months in Sanford, he reported directly to the two men who had interviewed him for the job, Capt. Roy and Sgt. Cote. On a typical assignment, they gave John the names of two suspects who regularly sold LSD and marijuana. John was to target both suspects and buy drugs from them.

Meanwhile, John and Peggy moved into a third-floor apartment that was perched over a small clothing store. The one-bedroom flat had a tiny living room and kitchenette.

"It was the dirtiest, worst place I have ever lived," John recalled. "The hallway stunk, but it was all I could afford." The apartment happened to be in close proximity to the two drug dealers that he was targeting.

John was concerned about Peggy's safety. He didn't want anyone to know where he lived, and he didn't want to attract any attention to Peggy. Therefore, when he went to work on the night shift, John would climb out the back window of his apartment and clambered down the fire escape.

He wandered the streets, trying to meet his two drug dealers. When he finally hooked up with them, he hung out, played pool with them, and even went to one of their apartments to play the guitar.

Through all this, John was alone with the two tough, tattooed biker types. He had no backup and no weapon. He had no contact with his captain or sergeant, nor was he wearing a wire or other communications device. "It was just me," he said, "out by myself on the streets, trying to buy drugs."

All of this was on-the-job training. "This was my first real experience with the drug scene," said John. "I had no training on how to buy drugs undercover."

During the next six weeks John tried to convince the suspects to sell him drugs, but no matter what he did or said, they refused. *Maybe they think, or know, that I'm a cop,* thought John. Whatever the reason, they didn't trust him. "I was too clean looking," John mused. "I didn't look like I used drugs. There were no scars or track marks on my arms. I couldn't really get close to them."

Eventually, Capt. Roy's patience wore thin. He couldn't

understand why John was unable to make a buy. John worried that his career was already over, and that Capt. Roy and Sgt. Cote had nothing good to say about him, other than that he was worthless. "And these were the two guys that hired me!" said John.

Fortunately John's first undercover gig didn't bury his burgeoning career. He needed training, so the department sent him to the police academy in Waterville, about six hours from Sanford.

Having been through army training and deployment, John was prepared to tackle the police academy's six-week military-style boot camp. He wasn't allowed to leave the campus, even on weekends. "We lived in old barracks that had a wood stove in the middle so we could keep warm," he recalled. "We even did PT [physical training] on the weekends."

The academy coursework was a rerun of John's experience at the Guam and MP training schools, so he sailed through the six weeks with ease. That was a good thing, because he had only one thing on his mind: getting through it and getting back home to his new wife.

Speaking of Peggy, while her husband was at the academy, she moved to the Arnold family farm in Milton and lived with John's parents, who had returned from Guam.

After John graduated from the Waterville academy, he rushed home and reunited with his wife. They went apartment hunting and found a little place that looked out onto the Mousam River. "It was particularly nice," said John, "compared to living over a clothing store. Things were looking up."

John's stint as an undercover cop was over, at least for now. It was time for him to wear yet another uniform—this time, the blues of a beat policeman—and start a new job. The Sanford police department assigned him to the night shift, headed by James Greaves, a patrol sergeant, whose brother Fred was also on the force.

In Vietnam, John had used an M16 rifle, a Colt .45 handgun, grenades and, when needed, a .50-caliber machine gun. Now he was back in the States, where the Sanford police department issued him a battered Smith & Wesson fixed-site revolver that was so old he could barely use it to qualify on the firing range. The gun was in such bad shape that John paid to have it reblued (redoing the protective finish on the steel). Fortunately, the department issued John a 12-gauge pump-action shotgun as a backup weapon.

To patrol the city streets, John drove a weathered Chevy Caprice. The car had double strobe bubble lights mounted on a bar across the roof, and a large siren-speaker bolted between the lights.

The department had only one dispatcher on duty. Sometimes John relieved the dispatcher so she could take her half-hour lunch.

"If you called in a license plate," recalled John, "they had an archaic system, using microfiche to look up the registered owner. Every month the state sent a current microfiche card that listed all of the license plates in the state. You stuck the card into the reader and looked through the magnifier, then scrolled down the list until you found the number that matched."

Most of the time, the officer making the stop would already have his information from the driver of the car before dispatch called back with it.

With all the fun he was having at work in the tiny police department, how could home life be any different? In October 1972, Peggy went into labor. She was in a lot of pain, and John did his best to help her.

"That was another eye-opener for me," said John. "I had never seen a child born. When Peggy went into labor, I drove us down to the hospital."

While the staff got Peggy situated on a bed in the hospital hallway—her room wasn't ready yet—John rang the attending physician, Dr. Richards, on the hallway phone. Dr. Richards said that he'd be right down. As John hung up, he heard someone shouting from behind him:

"Help!"

John whirled around. It was Peggy's scream. She was giving birth and there was no one qualified to help her along. But what John saw next horrified him even more.

Our new child has one foot sticking out!

John went into panic mode. "I started running around the halls in search of a doctor," he remembered. "Luckily, Dr. Richards showed up at about the same time."

Dr. Richards strolled alongside Peggy, who was still screaming in her bed in the hallway, and nodded.

"I guess it's time," he said.

Hospital staff wheeled Peggy into the delivery room, where John watched as Dr. Richards delivered a breached birth. Fortunately there were no further complications, and Peggy gave birth to a baby girl. John and Peggy named their new child Sandy Dee, after the actress Sandra Dee. "My wife liked to watch Sandra Dee movies," explained John.

Back on the job, John spent his first three years in the department—1972 to 1975—as a patrol officer. He handled all kinds of cases, from accidents to burglaries, and routine calls such as domestic disputes.

John was aggressive—a go-getter in every sense of the word. "I was always in the right place at the wrong time," said John. "In other words, I was always around when the bad guys were there." He was detail-oriented and looked under every rock he could find when he was chasing a case. For his by-the-book approach, his coworkers gave him the nickname "Straight Arrow."

"I would never take shortcuts or do anything that would violate department policy," noted John. "I would never back down from any situation, but I would always try to learn from every situation so that I could improve."

At shift change he turned his patrol car over to the officer who was relieving him, and vice versa. "You had to be careful to inspect the car not only for damage but also for contraband," he noted. "This is a standard police technique."

Criminals who were arrested, placed in the patrol car, and driven to the police station often attempted to hide contraband inside the car on the way so they weren't caught with it. "This might have been something that the arresting officer missed when he first searched the suspect," continued John. It was not uncommon to find knives or drugs under the backseat.

More than forty years later, even small incidents remain memorable. In one instance, John responded to a routine call: a dog had bitten a four-year-old girl, and the dog was still running loose in the city. "When I arrived," recalled John, "the dog attacked me, so I had to shoot and kill it."

At the time, John was unaware that he shouldn't shoot the dog in the head. The medical examiner needed the dog's brain intact so that it could be examined for a possible rabies infection. "Just another one of those little things I learned," said John," and would do better at next time."

For his crime-fighting efforts, John would become the most decorated officer in the Sanford police department during the 1970s. In 1983 he would receive the Jeremiah P. Sullivan Award from the New England Narcotics Officers' Association for his contributions to the field of drug enforcement.

There were a lot of domestic calls in Sanford. During one shift, John and his partner responded to a trailer home. To protect themselves, officers were taught not to stand in front of the door when knocking. Unfortunately, the mobile home had a tiny porch with a railing, and it was impossible for John to stand out of the way of the door.

When John knocked, the door opened, and a man greeted him with a 12-gauge shotgun that he jammed into John's stomach.

For some reason, the man didn't pull the trigger. John leaped to the side and chopped the shotgun with one hand. The side of the house had a six-foot drop. John fell and hit the ground hard.

As the suspect fled into the house, John and his partner scrambled back up the embankment, their guns trained on the front door.

"Drop your weapon and open the door!" John barked.

No word from inside the house…but no shotgun blast, either.

John and his partner shouted at the front door for the next five minutes, waiting for the suspect to respond. They called their dispatcher to ring the telephone inside the house. "Seemed like it took forever," recalled John.

Fortunately there was no gunfire. Eventually the suspect realized that he wasn't getting anywhere. He gave himself up and walked out the front door.

"That's an experience I'll never forget, and I still think about it occasionally," said John later. "It makes you think that you cheated death."

Toward the end of his stint as a patrol officer, John got a call at two o'clock in the morning. A man, armed with a gun, was burglarizing a small grocery store that was closed and locked up at that hour. "I was excited and scared at the same time," remembered John. "This was not the type of call where you go in with lights on and siren wailing. This was the type of call where you sneak in as quietly as possible to give yourself the position of advantage."

A backup officer, Arthur Titcomb, was just a few seconds behind John. As John approached the store in his patrol car, he saw a man outside, holding a long gun. John got on the radio.

"Man outside with a gun," he said.

Titcomb, the cover officer, pulled up on John's left. The two men drew their weapons and ordered the suspect to drop his gun.

Unfortunately the man with the long gun turned out to be the store owner, who'd been waiting for the police to arrive.

Oops.

Titcomb moved to the rear of the store to make sure the suspect didn't escape out the back. The officer peered through a back window of the store.

"Man in the store with a gun!" he yelled.

Meanwhile, the suspect dashed toward the front door.

John kicked the front door open just as the suspect rounded a corner inside and bolted toward the front of the store. John snapped on his flashlight and shone it around the dark shelves.

Titcomb entered the store the same way the suspect had, by crawling through a rear window, as John crept through the front door, waving his flashlight around.

John had the suspect in his flashlight beam.

"Stop and drop the gun, or you'll be shot!" yelled John.

The suspect complied, dropping his weapon, which clattered on the tile floor. Titcomb came up behind him, handcuffed the thief, and searched him. The thief was carrying a .44 Magnum revolver—fully loaded—and a hunting knife. The officers hauled the suspect off to jail.

In Maine, after an officer conducted a felony arrest, his case had to go before a grand jury to get an indictment to proceed to trial. The prosecuting attorney would question the arresting officer, who testified to the facts of the case. "This is similar to a preliminary hearing in some states," explained John. "In the case of a preliminary hearing, often called the prelim, it is generally the judge who decides if there is enough evidence to hold the suspect over for trial. But many states still use the grand jury system for this function." If the grand jury decided there was enough evidence to indict, then the case proceeded to trial.

In the case of the night store robber, the suspect was convicted and served two years in prison.

After three years on patrol duty, John was promoted to the rank of corporal in 1975. He was now second-in-command of the shift, and was usually the first backup officer on scene. If the sergeant was busy on a call or was off duty for the day, John would supervise the shift.

All officers in the Sanford police department were issued new weapons that year. "The new chrome-plated .357 Magnum revolvers were a step up from the fixed-sight Smith & Wessons we'd been using," recalled John. The officers also received speed loaders for the first time. Now if they found themselves in a gun battle, they could reload their weapons quickly.

Things were also looking up for John at home. He and Peggy had a second daughter, Susan, that year.

John transferred to the detective division, where he was a primary area investigator. For most police agencies, the area investigator or property crimes detective is the first job in a police officer's career after patrol. Area investigators work low-level street crimes of all types, including burglaries, robberies, assaults, domestic violence, and thefts. The next step up the career ladder is "specialized investigations" such as homicide, sex crimes, narcotics, and fraud. The job often comes with a take-home car and the additional perk of working the day shift with weekends off.

John had always been interested in taking college courses, so in 1976 he started work toward an associate's degree. "The Veterans Administration helped pay for the courses, which was good," said John, "because I was only making about $88 a week for being a police officer. At one point we applied for food stamps, but we got denied. With two kids, $88 a week didn't go far."

Sergeant John Arnold receives a citation for
heroism from the state legislature for rescuing a
boy from the icy Mousam River on December 28,
1977. Presenting the citation is Rep. David Paul
(D-Sanford). Photo by C. Scott Hoar of the
York County Journal Tribune.
JOHN ARNOLD COLLECTION

Chapter 8

THE BOY UNDER THE ICE

ON DECEMBER 28, 1977, John worked an incident that would not only become legend in the town of Sanford, but would also influence John and Peggy's marriage forever.

Due to shifting priorities, the Chief switched John back to patrol for a while. One day John got a call from the dispatcher: a child had gone missing. The child lived in a house next to the Mousam River, which ran through the middle of town.

Oh no, thought John. *Not the river.*

"I knew the place all too well," recalled John. "I knew that the river was frozen and that people were ice skating on top of it, but I also knew that there was a spot near the bridge that, because the current moved faster through it, never froze. The ice around this open area was thinner, and then got thicker as you moved outward to calmer spots on the river."

Maybe the child fell into the river.

On a hunch, John drove to the bridge and stopped near the middle. He jumped out of his patrol car and peered over the railing, down into the ice. He broke out in a cold sweat.

He could see something underneath the ice. It was small and looked like a child's body.

"I could see the ice skaters on the pond, a short distance away," John said. "I was thinking that the water current could take the child even deeper under the ice. I knew that my cover officer would be there in a minute or two, and that I could wait for him."

John decided not to wait. He unbuckled his gun belt and dropped it on the bridge. He stepped up on the railing and climbed over.

Out of the corner of his eye, he could see his cover officer running toward him on the bridge.

John took a deep breath, held it, and jumped into the river.

When John was a child, he couldn't swim. He was afraid of the water. But on that day, for some reason, he had no fear at all.

He landed feet first in the icy river. Chunks of ice floated all around him, and he saw the missing boy buried underneath the ice. John swam fifteen feet toward the boy, thankful that he'd slipped on his long johns that morning.

When he reached the boy, John took a breath and plunged underneath the ice, going down about three feet.

He saw the boy under the ice, floating, unconscious from the bitterly cold water. John grabbed the boy by the jacket and pulled him upward. They broke the surface of the water, and John gulped a lungful of air. He dragged the boy to shallow water that was about knee-deep.

"John!"

Looking up, John saw his cover officer shouting at him. It was Sgt. Cote, the shift supervisor. Cote waited on the bridge, holding a rope and with emergency equipment at the ready, in case he needed to hoist John out of the water. Bystanders and other officers on duty gathered nearby. Everyone on the bridge could see down to the ice where John was swimming.

As John pulled the body of the child to shore, Sgt. Cote ran over to assist. The two officers lay the boy on the shore and began mouth-to-mouth resuscitation. In the distance they heard the siren of an approaching ambulance.

The child was rushed to the emergency room, where a team of doctors worked on him for almost fourteen hours. The boy's name was Larry Davis, and he was just three years old.

Meanwhile, John was treated for exposure and released from the hospital. "I had not deteriorated into hypothermia," he recalled. "I think the long-john underwear helped me in some way."

Unfortunately the boy didn't survive the incident. He died at the hospital.

"It was a very sad day that I still think about from time to time," noted John later. "What could I have done differently? How long had the child been there? What were the parents thinking? I also think about the fact that I could have drowned that day."

Though John would later be honored for the rescue, it was a bittersweet experience. The rescue affected him profoundly, especially when it came to his feelings about children. When John and Peggy talked about the incident, John told his wife that he'd like to have another child, preferably a boy.

Mother Nature had other ideas, however, and a year or so later, John and Peggy welcomed their third daughter, Cheryl, into the world.

By 1977 John was considered a seasoned officer. He had been assigned to patrol duty, to the detectives, to the color guard, and was now back in the detective division, working burglary cases.

"I got to be a very good interviewer and became very good at convincing people to tell the truth," recalled John. "I would say to them, 'Tell the truth and shame the devil.' It was a saying I had picked up from my dad growing up."

Late that year, John finished his college courses and graduated with a two-year degree. He earned his sergeant's stripes the following year, but the promotion meant yet another round of rotation. As he remembered, "We worked eight days straight, off four days, then moved to a different shift. So we rotated shifts every twelve days. It really messed with your sleeping patterns, and as I got older it was more difficult. I didn't like leaving my daytime job in the detective division, but we served at the discretion of the Chief. You worked wherever he wanted you to work."

During one shift, John was outside of town and stopped a young couple for speeding. When they saw the lights flash on John's patrol car, the driver and passenger switched seats as they were driving. The man was now in the passenger seat, and the woman was behind the wheel. They stopped by the side of the road.

John pulled his patrol car in behind them and approached the passenger side of the vehicle. "I ended up at a disadvantage because I was standing in a small ditch," he said. "When I asked for the man's license, he reached back as if he was going to retrieve it, but instead he came out with his fist and coldcocked me in the face, knocking me backwards." John watched in frustration as the couple floored the accelerator and roared away.

However, as John always liked to say, "I don't back down much." He jumped back into his patrol car and took off after the fleeing vehicle.

"Somehow during the pursuit I was able to get in front of the vehicle and block it from the front, which is not the way they teach," John recalled. "The woman was still driving. I finally got them to stop."

The man got out of his car and approached John, who reached for the nightstick that was hanging from a loop in his gun belt.

Unfortunately John's hand grasped at air: he'd forgotten to bring his nightstick with him that day.

Well, doggone it, John thought to himself.

The male suspect—all six foot two and three hundred pounds of him—charged John.

"Stop!" John shouted. "Get on the ground!"

No luck. The man skidded to a halt in front of John, took up a boxing stance, and started to throw punches. John blocked several of them, and tackled the man to the ground.

The backup patrol car arrived just as the woman jumped out of the car. She had a large glass Pepsi bottle in her hand. She stepped to the front of her car and smashed the bottle across the hood, spitting shards of glass in all directions. As John's backup officer stepped out of his patrol car, the woman marched toward him, holding the jagged broken bottle in front of her as a weapon.

Meanwhile, the male suspect was still throwing punches at John, who pulled his .357 Magnum revolver out of its holster.

"Stop this right now," said John, "or I'm gonna shoot you."

John had no intention of firing his weapon; he was hoping to gain the man's cooperation.

"Well," said the man, "shoot me, then."

That wasn't quite the response that John was hoping to hear, so he reholstered his gun and continued fighting with his hands. The two men rolled on the ground, grappling at each other in the dirt.

John recalled the scene vividly: "I was now bear wrestling on the ground with this guy, and it was exhausting. No mace. No nightstick. A third cop was able to turn the guy over. We used two sets of handcuffs to get his arms behind his back to hook him up. I was bleeding a little—facial cuts, a minor nosebleed, that kind of thing."

The woman eventually gave up trying to use her Pepsi bottle as a weapon, and the officers took both suspects into custody. Then they noticed that there was a small child in the suspects' car.

"As I recall," John continued, "we only had four officers working day shift back then. We had to find someone to watch the child in the car as we took mom and dad away to jail." Then John drove to the hospital, where medical staff attended to his injuries from the fight.

The male suspect was charged with felony assault on a peace officer. He went to trial, where the judge sentenced him to six months of jail time.

When the man had completed his sentence, he phoned John.

"I'd like to meet with you," he told John. "Alone."

John didn't like what he was hearing. "I'm thinking the worst," he recalled. "I was thinking that this guy just wanted to do me in. But me being me, I agreed to meet with him. Of course I told one of my fellow officers where I would be, and that if he didn't hear from me in a short time, he'd better start checking on me."

Unsure of how the suspect might behave, John decided on an open, public place to meet: the parking lot of the local Ames department store.

They two men approached each other cautiously.

"Look," said the man, "I'm really sorry about what happened.

When you stopped me, I'd just been arguing with my wife. I never meant for things to get so bad."

John nodded. It was nice for the man to tell him this, but John wasn't about to trust him.

"I respect you," continued the man, "for standing up to me. For going round and round with me, and for not shooting me."

"Okay," said John, "thanks."

"If you need anything in the future, just let me know, and I'll help you out."

Bingo. Now John knew what this was all about. The man had just volunteered to be an informant.

The man hung out at the Wolf Club, a local bar. "When problems happened there," said John, "he was one of the guys who would look at me, give me a nod, and eventually bring out the guy causing the problem.

"I guess even bad guys can sort of become good guys," mused John, "if there is even a little bit of mutual respect."

Chapter 9

DRUG BUYS

DURING THE EARLY 1980s, John worked a lot of dope cases out of the detective division. Using tips provided by informants, John set up and supervised drug-buying operations.

The undercover police officers who bought the drugs needed to be unfamiliar to the locals in Sanford, so the police department sometimes borrowed officers from other agencies or from out of state. For one case, the Sanford PD brought in an officer from Rochester, New Hampshire. John talked the officer through the procedure.

"We'd have the informant introduce him to a few drug dealers," said John. "Then the informant would be out of the picture, and the undercover cop would just start making drug buys. We'd come a long way as a department since I was roaming the streets as a rookie cop, trying to buy drugs!"

During his early days with the department, John had been on his own. He had none of the resources that the newer undercover cops were receiving. He never wore a wire, nor did he have a surveillance team or safety officers nearby to assist.

By the early 1980s, the Sanford police department made sure that undercover cops were wired all the time, using a device known as the "black box." The four-inch-by-four-inch square device was taped to the undercover officer's chest or back—"just like you see on TV," noted John. "There was always a safety officer or team nearby. We could then hear the conversation within a certain distance—generally about a half a mile—and we would know if things started going bad."

Most of the undercover buys were for marijuana or cocaine, about an ounce or so. Street price for an ounce of marijuana was twenty-five dollars, while a speedball (cocaine mixed with heroin or morphine, then injected) ran twenty-five to thirty-five dollars.

After the undercover officer made the purchase, John and other officers met him later and logged the drugs as evidence. After about twelve purchases, the department would shut down the operation and go to the grand jury to get indictments.

John's informant at the Wolf Club—the man John had almost shot during a traffic stop gone wild—proved a useful source of information. The informant called John one day and passed along the word:

"I'll put you in touch with the dealer," said the informant. "He's from out of state, and he's trying to sell two pounds of marijuana."

At the time, two pounds was a lot of marijuana, and the Sanford cops didn't want it hitting the streets. John put on civilian clothes and headed down to the Wolf Club. He got on the phone with the dealer, presenting himself as a potential buyer, and the haggling ensued.

"I want fifteen hundred dollars a pound," said the dealer.

"That's three thousand bucks!" said John. "I don't have that kind of money."

John eventually talked the dealer down to one thousand dollars per pound. They arranged to meet in the parking lot of the Ames department store. As John recalled, "We had no real money to use as buy money, so we had to scramble around and scrape together a few hundred dollars. We cashed that into a bunch of dollar bills, so we had a big stack of money, with a couple of hundred-dollar bills on top of the stack."

When the police were staged around the department store parking lot, John made the call to the dealer.

"I'm here," said John. "I'm in my pickup truck. It's green."

John had always hated the color of that green truck, but he was a bargain hunter and had bought it at half price, which made the color more tolerable.

"How will I know it's you?" continued John.

"I have a long red beard," said the dealer, "and I'm driving a new blue Ford car."

The dealer arrived, swapped his drugs for the roll of bills, and started to drive away. Sanford police officers halted the dealer's vehicle and arrested him. In addition to retrieving the money, the police retrieved two guns.

Anytime you can get dope and guns off the street and put a doper in jail, it's a good day, thought John.

As John gained more experience working drug deals, the Sanford police department relied on him to execute cocaine and marijuana busts. "I became the go-to operational person," he said. "I set up the drug buys as far as surveillance techniques and background checks on suspects, did all of the homework, and figured out if the dealers were local or someone out of state. I would check with outside agencies, including DEA."

Most of the department buys were marijuana and cocaine, on a small scale. "The two pounds of marijuana we got earlier was a pretty big deal to us," said John. "We were mostly buying a couple ounces of marijuana and maybe a gram of coke at the time. The drugs were out there, but I guess we didn't realize how much dope was available on the streets at the time."

John saw many of the same faces over and over again. "Every time we busted these people, we would interview them and try to gather more information about the drug business in the Sanford area," recalled John. "We wanted to know where the drugs were coming from, and what channels they used to bring the drugs in."

John was fast becoming an expert at putting together and working drug cases and undercover narcotic operations. This knowledge would serve him well in the future.

The people at the Sanford Airport were very nice and always had coffee on, so John had made it part of his regular routine to stop in and say hello.

In April 1981 John drove out to the airport to talk to the manager and deliver a verbal thank-you from the police department. "They had recently helped us out by providing an airplane and a pilot, free of charge, to help us track down a bank robber," John recalled. "I wanted to drive out and thank them personally."

During the visit, a flight instructor pulled John aside.

"Sergeant Arnold, I really need to talk to you."

John directed the instructor to a far corner of a building, where the two men could talk without being interrupted. The instructor glanced around, nervous, and said:

"There's, uh, suspicious activity going on around here."

John nodded. "And?"

"Well, if you…um, if you look carefully at some of the planes here, you'll notice that some of them…well, some of them have green residue on the propellers."

"Green residue?" said John.

"Yeah," said the instructor. "It's probably because the planes are landing in fields that have tall grass. So the propellers are churning around in the grass when the planes land or take off."

"Any specific aircraft you can tell me about?" said John.

The instructor shrugged. "I really can't…" he trailed off.

"I understand," said John. "Thanks for letting me know."

After that cryptic conversation, John decided to hang out at the airport whenever he could. Sometimes he showed up in uniform, and sometimes he arrived in street clothes. He hung out with pilots, mechanics, administrative staff—anyone he could chat with and possibly learn more about the airplanes stained with green.

During his visits, John learned a bit about aviation and the operation of an airport. "I had no idea that a tail number on an airplane could be run through a database, just like a license plate on a vehicle," he recalled. "This was a real revelation to me, because I realized I could run the tail number of a plane, find out who owned it, and then run his name through more national databases to see if he'd been arrested before, or what type of criminal record he had."

John also used his time at the airport to sharpen his skills at developing informants, learning how to talk to people, and trying to be a better cop.

Eventually the instructor pilot directed John to a specific plane. It was a high-wing, single-engine, four-seat Cessna 172, and it had the giveaway green stains on its propeller.

John and the instructor pilot called the FAA and ran the tail number through the registry, which was public information. The plane was registered to a company (later revealed to have a false name) in Connecticut. The name on the registration was Michael Sanborn.

As a courtesy, the FAA alerted DEA regarding the call, and DEA talked briefly with the Sanford police department. "DEA was only interested in the fact that the plane was in Sanford," recalled John. "Why? Because Michael Sanborn had a prior drug arrest in Connecticut. DEA asked us to contact them if we developed anything from it."

John followed up on the information and learned that Sanborn lived five miles away in North Berwick, which bordered Sanford to the south.

However, Sanborn wasn't a licensed pilot. That meant someone else was flying the plane in and out of the airport.

John's quick stop at the airport to say "thanks" was turning into a one-man surveillance operation. He started collecting license plate numbers. He watched vehicles that drove around the airport to pick up passengers. He started collecting names. Most of the people lived in Sanford. Some had criminal records.

"At this point," said John, "we were just at the investigation stage, mostly surveillance, trying to figure out what activity they were involved in." John and his supervisor, Capt. Ruel, talked about calling in the state police or the DEA to assist. Unfortunately, budget cuts were forcing agencies to shutter their ongoing antidrug operations. The suspicious activity in Sanford was just that: suspicious. Since John hadn't been able to connect the suspects with drug-smuggling activity, he didn't have a case yet.

Nevertheless, John continued his trips to the airport, and the Sanford police collected more names and information. Then John had some good luck. "I ran a tail number on one airplane, and it had been red-flagged by the DEA," he recalled. "Suddenly they were calling us about this plane. They wanted to know if it was at the airport."

Next, the Sanford police hosted meetings with the DEA and the state police. Everyone was having budget problems. The state police smuggling unit was in danger of being shut down. "But," added John, "we now had the attention of other agencies, and this is when the case really started to grow."

Chapter 10

TWO SHIFTS A DAY

In the middle of this snowballing activity, Chief Pride retired from the Sanford police department. His replacement, Arthur Kelly, was a smart, tough man from Massachusetts. Kelly decided to rotate some of his officers, and John Arnold got word that he was moving from the detective division to—yet again—patrol division. However, this time John would be a supervisor.

John and Capt. Ruel asked for a meeting with the new chief. They briefed him on the activity at the airport, their surveillance of Michael Sanborn and his friends, and their discussions with the DEA and the state police.

"Chief, this could be a really big case," said John.

Chief Kelly nodded. "I hear you, John, but I need you in patrol. I need a strong supervisor on the streets. We're having problems with some officers not following standard procedure. Nighttime burglaries are increasing, and our people aren't doing the nighttime business checks like they're supposed to."

John was known as a strict, by-the-book supervisor. As he put it: "I was all business on my watch, but everyone went home safe at the end of the night."

"I know it's not what you want," continued Chief Kelly, "but I need you there, and I need you there *now*."

John and Capt. Ruel tried on several occasions to convince Chief Kelly of the importance of their burgeoning case, but the chief stood firm. However, he did give them some leeway: they could continue working the case, but only outside of their normal duty hours.

"That was all we needed to hear," said John. "From this point on, we didn't inform anyone else on the department about the case. The only people who knew about the investigation were Capt. Ruel, the new chief, and me. We didn't want anyone else on the department to know about it, for fear that word of the investigation would accidentally filter back to some of the suspects involved in the case."

Based on the investigation so far, John knew that Michael Sanborn was the main player in a group of several local people. In his office, John placed a large sheet of paper on a table. He pulled a quarter out of his pocket and dropped it onto the center of the paper. With a pencil he traced the quarter, then wrote Sanborn's name in the resulting circle.

John and Capt. Ruel drew lines extending outward, and continued to trace the quarter to add the names of Sanborn's suspected associates.

It was a low-tech but effective way to illustrate the case they were building, but the case had too many players and not enough relationships established. John wanted to see how all of the people were related to each other. "We continued this circle graph and connected people through several layers," explained John. "Sometimes the lines and circles with names would go down three or four levels, and that third or fourth person would then connect back to Sanborn."

Who was Michael Sanborn? The mysterious would-be aerial drug smuggler was around thirty years old and lived in a secluded, wooded area in North Berwick. His home was a large, beautiful log cabin, worth $150,000, that sat far off the road.

The Sanford police department stepped up its surveillance of the Sanborn home. "We started doing some drive-bys to check out the location and the layout," recalled John, who also investigated the house while on foot. He and a female officer, Gloria, would take "strolls" in the woods behind the Sanborn cabin. During their walks, John checked the cabin for counter-surveillance equipment such as cameras and booby traps.

"Gloria was my cover," said John. "If we were seen or someone came up to us, we could say that we were just out for a walk, looking for mushrooms in the woods or something." Gloria was kept in the dark about the specifics of the case. Again, only the chief and Capt. Ruel had full knowledge of the investigation.

John noticed that a lot of cars drove through the Sanborn property. Sometimes people would park and go inside; at other times the cars would stop for only a short time. Many of the drivers spent time at the Washington Square Restaurant, a local diner in Sanford.

"Everything was tying together as far as all the players and where they spent their time: the airport, the Washington Square Restaurant, and Sanborn's property," said John. "We were now pretty confident that Sanborn was the center of whatever was going on, and that he was the person we needed to be watching most of the time."

With Sanborn now the focus of the investigation, John did his best to keep track of him at all times, whether Sanborn was at home, at the airport, or being flown somewhere in his airplane. John continued hammering away at the case after his regular eight-hour shift as a patrol supervisor, as the new chief had allowed him to do.

Many officers would be exhausted after a full workday, but John's interest in the case gave him an extra shot of energy. Chief Kelly's arrangement—that John could work the case after completing his daily shift in the patrol division—actually worked out well in terms of continuing the case.

Because John was able to travel wherever he needed during his patrol shift, he was able to keep an eye on Sanborn, to some extent, while performing his other duties. "I would note when

Sanborn was at the restaurant," said John, "and I would keep track of some of his movements when I could, including what vehicle he was in, whether he was picked up in a vehicle, and things like that."

Chapter 11

FIRST CONTACT

JOHN ARNOLD CHECKED his watch and let out a long breath. It was 11:00 p.m. on November 9, 1981. Temperatures outside were near freezing, and John had the motor running in his patrol car so he could keep the heater going. He was parked near the police station.

Several hours ago, Michael Sanborn had sauntered into the Washington Square Restaurant, just down the street. He hadn't come out yet. John knew that Sanborn would probably drive past the police station on his way home to North Berwick. John lay in wait.

The guy is taking forever to come back out, thought John.

To move the case forward, it was time for John to form a relationship with Michael Sanborn.

An hour later, Sanborn drove by in his 1977 Chevy pickup. The truck had a maroon paint job with a white cap on the back, which made it easy to spot. John released the parking brake in his patrol car and rolled into the traffic lane, following Sanborn from a distance.

Sanborn's car weaved back and forth, crossed over the centerline, and came back into his lane.

He's had a few too many, thought John, who was hoping for a reason to pull a traffic stop. Sanborn had given John the perfect reason. John snapped on his lights and whooped his siren once. Ahead of him, Sanborn's car slowed and pulled to the side of the road.

John stepped out of his patrol car and approached Sanborn's vehicle. He halted just behind the open driver's window and shined his flashlight inside. Sanborn blinked at him several times.

"'Evening, officer," said Sanborn. He was alone in the car. His speech was a little slushy.

"Sir," John said, "may I see your driver's license, please?"

Sanborn fumbled for his wallet, yanked his license out, and handed it to John.

John nodded. "Sir, you appear to be driving under the influence of alcohol."

Sanborn was quiet. John pretended to study the license for a moment. Then he looked at Sanborn and said something unusual:

"Look, Mr. Sanborn, I'm a pretty nice guy. From looking at your address here, you don't live too far away. Tell you what. I'm not gonna cuff you. I'm at the end of my shift, and you just need to get home. I'll follow you to your house to make sure you get there without any more hassles. Okay?"

Sanborn looked a little surprised. He nodded.

They drove to his house, John following Sanborn into the New Berwick woods. They rolled up to Sanborn's giant cabin and got out of their cars. Two German Shepherds guarded the property.

John looked at the cabin. "Hell," he muttered, "I couldn't afford this place on my salary, that's for sure."

The two men chatted about a few mundane things, and then John turned toward his patrol car.

"I have to go," said John. "But if you ever need anything, give me a call at the police department and I'll try to help you out."

As John drove away, he took a deep breath. *Okay,* he thought. *So this is how it all begins.*

Chapter 12

PROXIMITY

Now THAT HE'D made a connection to the supposed drug-running operation, John had to exploit that connection. He had to get closer to Michael Sanborn. He had to figure out a reason to go to Sanborn's house—a reason to hang out there.

If I can do this, thought John, *I'll be in a good position to watch license plates on cars that come and go at the house. I can see people's faces up close, and maybe get to know them.*

John's solution? He'd offer to cut firewood.

Dressed in civilian clothes, John drove to the cabin in his personal pea-green Ford pickup truck. As he pulled into Sanborn's driveway, one of Sanborn's German Shepherds barked at him.

Sanborn strolled down the driveway and met John at the truck. They talked about the trees lining the driveway.

"I thought that maybe I could help you cut some firewood," said John. "I was looking for something to do, and you're out here in the woods, and I figured...well, I figured that I could help out."

On that first visit, John avoided talking about his "personal problems." But when he visited on another day, he and Sanborn talked more about themselves. Sanborn asked John about the life of a cop.

"Money problems," John grumbled. "Cops don't get paid much."

Sanborn said that he'd moved to Maine from Connecticut. John talked about his upbringing in New Hampshire. He complimented Sanborn on his beautiful log cabin.

"I dream of owning a house someday," said John. "I have three kids and a wife that I can barely afford. I gotta pay for food and the heating bill." He gestured at the trees. "That's why I wanted to chop firewood. I can burn it and save money on the electric bill."

Sanborn handed John a beer. John pretended to be very thankful, poor as he was supposed to be.

"You know," John added, "when the staff officers at the station go home at 5:00 p.m., the whole town of Sanford is my responsibility. After five, I control the town, in a way. But they just don't pay me enough for all the headaches I have to deal with."

Sanborn nodded. "Why don't you come back in a few days, and we'll go out back and do some chopping?"

John thanked Sanborn, and returned to police headquarters to sit down with Capt. Ruel.

"Okay," said Capt. Ruel. "He knows you're a cop. He knows that you're friendly and that you gave him a break."

John and Capt. Ruel reviewed the possibilities. *What could happen? What are the dangers involved? How far could this go?*

At the time, John wasn't thinking about infiltrating Sanborn's group. John's role as a crooked cop was, so far, to obtain information that could be helpful in building a bigger case. To do that, John had to be visible to Sanborn on a regular basis, and he needed to continue giving Sanborn the idea that he knew everyone and everything going on, because it was "his town."

John considered driving by Sanborn's cabin, but since the house was in the next town over and was set back from the road by a five-hundred-foot driveway, Sanborn would never see him rolling by. Instead, said John, "I would make it a point to see him in town, so I could make him think that I was always around. I spent a lot of time on the phone with him. I'd drive by and wave at him, even when I was in my patrol car. Sanborn would wave back."

After several weeks, John realized that he had to expand his undercover role. He had to fully become the part he was playing. It would be difficult for him. He had never been a man to keep secrets—after all, his nickname was Straight Arrow—and he was never a wild kind of guy in his off-duty hours. He had a family. Peggy and his three daughters were his world.

"This was a small-town police agency, so everyone knew everyone," John continued. "As police officers, we would hang out together quite often, go to police parties together, and things like that. In the past, I had never been the type to go out and go barhopping. But I saw that my role had to change if I was going to be successful at this case."

During the next several months, John slowly and carefully altered his image. He hung out at bars until 2:00 a.m., drinking and chatting up the regulars. His crisp, poised demeanor slowly cracked; he looked like he cared less and less about his appearance and his job performance. Word got around the department, and his police buddies asked him what was going on.

"Oh, nothing," he told them. "My wife and I are having problems. I got a lot of stress. If you see me in a club, don't come over and talk to me. Just leave me alone. That's all I want, okay?"

John's undercover role made him an outcast and the talk of the department. Many of his colleagues thought he was losing it. The gig was a psychological minefield for John as well: "There were times that I wondered, myself, if I was going off the deep end," he said.

As John later recalled: "I knew that this type of investigation was unusual. Here I was, a uniformed patrol sergeant, doing my best to infiltrate a drug-smuggling ring, as a known cop. I had to play both sides, which is unusual in a drug investigation. Most cops just go undercover, and all of their cop buddies know that they're working narcs and are undercover. So the honesty and integrity of the undercover cop is never questioned. But in my case, none of my fellow officers knew that I was taking on a covert role."

The case was also hard on his marriage. He and Peggy came close to splitting up. Although Peggy had a basic understanding of what was going on, she would still spend nights waiting up for John, only to see him stumble through the front door in the wee hours, smelling like smoke and beer.

"What the hell are you doing to yourself?" she would ask.

"Peggy, please," he would answer. "You just have to trust me. Trust that I am doing the right thing. This is going to be a big case."

John was working an eight-hour shift in uniform from 2:00 p.m. until 10:00 p.m. From 10:00 p.m. until 3:00 or 4:00 a.m. he was in street clothes, hanging out with Michael Sanborn.

John would later say that the only reason his marriage stayed intact was because his wife was so strong. "It was a time in our life that could have gone either way, both in my marriage and in my personal life," he recalled. "There were opportunities for me to go the wrong way and actually become what I was pretending to be."

From November through March, John continued to call Sanborn on the phone and stop by the cabin frequently. John offered Sanborn assistance, a shoulder to cry on, and a dirty cop friend who was also an eager student regarding the drug trade. On many of his visits to the Sanborn home, John saw two women, one of whom was Sanborn's girlfriend.

On January 12, 1982, John's relationship with Sanborn got closer. John received a phone call at home from the police department. The reason? Sanborn was in the hospital. He had just been involved in a traffic accident, and he may have killed someone. Sanborn had crossed the yellow line and drove into oncoming traffic.

John rushed to the hospital. Although he was concerned about possible victims, he also needed to sustain the ongoing investigation. Unfortunately, his main contact might have just blown everything wide open.

Because he was a police sergeant, John was able to enter Sanborn's room and speak to him before anyone else. Sanborn lay in a hospital bed, white sheets covering him. He had an IV in his arm, and he was in quite a bit of pain. As John recalled later, "I wasn't there to confront him, since I was his pal. He looked sad, but when he saw me, he perked up."

John walked to the side of the bed and said, "Michael, I'm sorry this happened. I'm here as a friend. If you need anything, let me know."

Sanborn nodded. "I think I'll probably be charged with a crime. I hit someone, and he may be dead."

"If the traffic officer wants to talk to you, don't say anything to him. Ask for a lawyer. Don't talk to the police."

John gave Sanborn the names of several attorneys. Looking back later, John would view this incident as the point where Sanborn truly began to trust him. The drug investigation was just as important as the investigation into the accident. Of course, John couldn't tell anyone except his supervisor, Capt. Ruel.

Ultimately the other driver died of his injuries, and Sanborn was charged with vehicular manslaughter. The police investigator was incensed when he found out that John had slipped in to talk to Sanborn at the hospital. Unfortunately, John couldn't reveal that he was undercover. The investigator complained to Chief Kelly, who talked to John behind closed doors.

"You're doing everything smartly," said the chief, "and everything you need to do. So keep doing what you're doing, John."

After Sanborn returned home from the hospital, he phoned John at the police department and asked him to meet. John dropped by Sanborn's cabin.

"How does all this work?" said Sanborn. "Will I be arrested?"

"Not necessarily," said John. "You'll get an attorney. Bail will be set, and a court date scheduled for a later time."

As they were talking, John noticed a parking ticket lying next to the telephone. The time on the ticket was 2:00 a.m. that day. John peered at the name of the vehicle owner that was written on the ticket: RICHARD STRATTON.

Now that's a coincidence, thought John. *I issued that ticket myself, in front of the Washington Square Restaurant. Why is the ticket here, in Michael Sanborn's home?*

When he returned to the station, John saw the long faces of his fellow officers. Because John had visited Sanborn in the hospital, the entire department now knew that the two men were connected. As John recalled later, "You know how cops are.

When they find out that another cop—who had nothing to do with the accident investigation—was at the hospital and was talking to the suspect, the word spreads all over the department. People were asking, 'What's John Arnold doing with this guy?'"

The situation didn't get any better. The accident investigation soon revealed that Sanborn had cocaine in his bloodstream during the accident. Now John's fellow officers were asking, "Why is John Arnold hanging out with a guy who's doing cocaine?"

John experienced a lot of lonely moments during that period. "I had to befriend Michael Sanborn," he noted, "and at the same time, I had to lie to my fellow officers about what I was doing. On top of all that, I had to tell my wife almost nothing about what I was doing, for fear that she might slip up and tell one of the other officers' spouses, which could cause problems with the case, or cause an issue for me.

"I had to do everything I could to protect the relationship I was building with Michael Sanborn, and I had to protect the integrity of the investigation. Unfortunately, this meant hiding the truth from almost everyone except Capt. Ruel and the Chief."

Meanwhile, John was also keeping an eye on the Sanford airport. He was getting burned out working long shifts. John had spent a lot of time developing his relationship with Michael Sanborn, but he wasn't sure if the case would develop into a bigger one. *Are we going to get anything out of this*, thought John, *after all of the time we've put into it?*

Chapter 13

THE SETUP

ON JANUARY 21, 1982—a clear night, with the air crisp and cold—John and Capt. Ruel headed to the airport to do a drive-by. They were in an unmarked detective car, a Ford Maverick that had no emergency lights. They had only a hand-held radio to communicate with the department.

When John and Capt. Ruel neared the airfield, they saw a van that appeared to be heading directly for the hangar where Michael Sanborn kept his aircraft.

"We parked in a wooded area that was known as a make-out spot for the local guys and girls," said John. "The spot gave us a good view of the hangar." They had previously scouted the area in case they'd need to do surveillance.

The lights inside the hangar were on, giving John and Capt. Ruel a clear view of what was happening inside. John checked his watch. It was 3:00 a.m.

Four people walked into the hangar. John, peering through his binoculars, saw Michael Sanborn and another man whom he would later learn was Richard Stratton, the leader of the smuggling operation.

The airplane was towed onto the parking ramp. It was a Beechcraft Sport 150, not the Cessna 172 that John had seen previously.

The engine spun up, and soon the airplane taxied out—in total darkness, as the pilot didn't switch on the aircraft lights—and trundled toward the runway. The aircraft picked up speed and took off, disappearing into the night. Later, John would check and find out that the Beechcraft was headed to Canada.

In the dark, it was difficult to make out what was going on. "I believe only Sanborn and the pilot flew to Canada that night," John noted later. "Stratton and the other person disappeared."

Several hours later, the Beechcraft returned to Sanford Airport.

The next day, John updated the DEA, which was now very interested in what was going on. They wanted to know more about what Richard Stratton was doing, and they wanted to know why his airplane had flown to Canada and back. As John recalled, "From that point on, the DEA helped us with whatever we needed. They became involved in the surveillance and provided all of the recording devices. They also ran surveillance on me when I met with Michael Sanborn. Often I knew that DEA had people watching me."

Several weeks later, on a cold Thursday evening in February, John stepped through the door of the Washington Square tavern in Sanford. Michael Sanborn was already there, sitting at a table in the back. There weren't a lot of customers in the place, which afforded Sanborn and John some privacy. They played Pac-Man to see who could get the higher score.

The two men ordered drinks, and Sanborn chatted about his fifteen-year career smuggling marijuana and hashish in Vermont, Connecticut, and now Maine. John leaned in, appearing to soak in Sanborn's tales of cash-and-carry. John needed to come across as a cop ready to make some extra bucks.

Sanborn raised his glass and swallowed a mouthful of beer. He slid the glass back onto the tabletop and spread his arms. "You know, John, you're sitting in my pub? I put twenty thousand dollars into this place."

"I'm impressed," said John. "I couldn't put twenty dollars into this place. How do you afford all this?"

Sanborn smiled and tapped his temple. "I'm smart. And"— his voice got softer—"I run a little cocaine along with the other stuff."

"A bigger moneymaker than pot," said John.

"Yeah. Plus," laughed Sanborn, "I got some marijuana plants growing up in the attic of my house."

John smiled. "Always good to have a backup plan, huh? Anyway, what's with your airplane? You keep talking about selling it, but here you are making runs to Canada in it."

"I did sell it," said Sanborn. "There's a guy in Texas who has an Aero Commander that I'm gonna buy. It can carry somewhere from fifteen hundred to two thousand pounds of marijuana at a time. That's almost a full thousand pounds more than my old Beechcraft!"

John didn't say anything. Sanborn was on a roll.

"Couple of weeks ago, this guy from Phillips flew with me to Canada," said Sanborn. "We get up there, and can you believe it? The pilot refuses to land the fucking thing!"

John forced himself not to react. He and Capt. Ruel had watched the same aircraft take off from the Sanford Airport several weeks prior, but he didn't know that Stratton had been aboard.

"What," said John, "you have cops waiting for you or something?"

Sanborn shook his head. "I say to the pilot, 'Put us on the ground.' And the pilot's whining, 'The wings have started to ice up. I don't think I can land safely.' You believe it? A six-hundred-mile round trip to Canada, a little ice, and the asshole says he can't land? So we had to turn back."

"You brought the drugs back?"

"Yes," said Sanborn. "Richard is pissed at me, and he's pissed at the pilot." Sanborn rubbed his hands together. "John," he said,

"I'm putting together the biggest deal I've ever been involved in. Get this: it'll have some hashish, some marijuana, and some coke. It's all waiting at an airport down in South Carolina."

Sanborn planned to have several trucks or vans inside the hangar in South Carolina. When his airplane landed there, it would take ten to fifteen minutes to load the cargo and take off.

"How much cargo?" asked John.

"Oh, maybe 1,500 to 2,000 pounds of marijuana. It's coming from outside the country."

"And after you get it back here to Sanford?"

"We have several stash houses around here where we can store the stuff."

John nodded. "So," he said, "what do you need me to do?"

"You're on patrol duty, right? So you take care of our, ah, security at the Sanford Airport. Watch out for the DEA. If you see them around town or around the airport, you let us know right away. You're driving around in your patrol car anyway, so nobody will think anything's unusual."

Sanborn was still being cautious and asked John if he was wearing a wire. John headed to the bathroom to take off his shirt, but Sanborn changed his mind. (John wasn't wired at the time, fortunately.)

"Do you know any people who work in drug enforcement or law enforcement?" said Sanborn.

"Yes," said John. "I know some."

"I'll pay you. How's a thousand dollars sound?"

"What's it for?"

"Strictly for security of the airport."

They agreed on that amount and left the restaurant. John drove them to the Sanborn home. Sanborn disappeared inside while John sat in his truck with the motor running.

After a few minutes, Sanborn came back outside and slipped John an envelope.

"That's a thousand in cash," Sanborn explained. "After the first load goes through Sanford Airport, you'll get five thousand more."

John nodded and shoved the envelope into his coat pocket.

"Remember, John, you have to let me know when the DEA is wandering around town, or when they're stalking the airport. That's what we're paying you for. You're our security guy."

"I got it," said John.

"I'm gonna talk to my main man," Sanborn continued. "He's in Phillips. Maybe I can get you an additional percentage from him. Sound good?"

John nodded again.

"You okay with all this? You look a little nervous."

"I'm okay," said John. "It's not like I've done this before. But I'll do what you want."

Sanborn grinned and pointed at the envelope in John's pocket. "Enjoy that, my friend. You'll be able to buy a lot of shit for yourself once we get this going."

Sanborn headed back inside. John waited until Sanborn shut the front door, then drove slowly to police headquarters, where he turned the envelope of cash—now evidence in the case—over to Capt. Ruel.

Chapter 14

THE REST OF THE RING

BUILDING A CASE against Sanborn and the rest of the smuggling operation would take time. The thousand dollars was the first building block in what would become a gigantic stack of evidence.

Three weeks later, on February 23, John and Sanborn gathered, again, at the Washington Square Restaurant in Sanford. It was midafternoon, and John was hoping that Sanborn would give him more details about how the drugs were smuggled across the U.S.-Canada border.

"I just came back from Michigan with six or seven boxes of hashish," Sanborn boasted.

John, playing naïve, asked Sanborn what hashish was.

"You really don't know, do you?" Sanborn chuckled. He squared his fingers at the knuckles to represent a box that measured about one foot square. "Looks like this."

John gently pushed for more information. "So what do you make from moving this stuff?"

"For hashish, I'm getting seven hundred fifty dollars per pound. If I sell it in Canada, I get a thousand per pound. I just carried $750,000 of the stuff down to Florida."

Sanborn started preaching to John about loyalty and trust and how they were both a part of the business.

That's funny, John thought to himself. *Honor among thieves.*

Sanborn continued: "And if you see any of our people while you're out driving around town in your patrol car—"

"I'll give them a break," said John.

Sanborn nodded. "Good."

"When do I become a real part of all this?" said John. "Right now I'm just helping you out."

"I don't know yet. Could be this week, next week, or a month from now. But"—Sanborn smiled from ear to ear—"when it rains, it pours!"

John took a sip of his drink. "How are you going to contact me when it's time to go?"

"One of us will call the police station and ask for you," said Sanborn. "We'll tell them our name is Linda or David, and ask you to call us back. Those will be our 'code names': Linda or David. That'll mean you need to get a hold of me right away."

Ever so gently, John needed to nudge Sanborn toward arranging a meeting with the boss, Richard Stratton.

"Have you talked to the man in Phillips?" said John.

Sanborn nodded. "In fact, he may be around today. Would you like to meet him?"

"Sure," said John.

"Hey, one other thing," said Sanborn. "The DEA. Are their people around town? And if they are, can you find out when?"

John leaned back in the booth.

"Absolutely."

Chapter 15

ON THE WIRE

Two DAYS LATER, on February 25, 1982, Sanborn asked John to visit the cabin. It was time for John to meet some of the members of Sanborn's group.

John drove his Ford pickup to the cabin. Underneath his shirt was a tape recorder that was fastened to his skin. He parked the pickup and gently pushed the power button on the recorder. As he did so, Sanborn strolled out of the cabin and said hello.

"Got some people inside for you to meet," grinned Sanborn. He introduced a man and two women, one of whom was his girlfriend, Linda Prior. Everyone sat down for a chat.

"Speaking of people," said Sanborn, "did you get a chance to check out that guy whose name I gave you?" Sanborn had asked John to run motor vehicle and criminal history checks to see if the police were watching another member of the group.

"He's fine." John paused. "What about the other name you gave me? Richard Stratton?"

"Yeah," said Sanborn. "I need you to check him out too. He's about thirty-six years old." Sanborn grabbed a piece of paper and wrote a name on it: RICHARD LOWELL STRATTON. He handed the piece of paper to John, who folded it and put it in his pocket.

"One other thing," said Sanborn. He pulled an ink pen from his pocket and handed it to John. The pen was marked with the name RAMADA INN.

"I stole it from the hotel today," Sanborn said, smiling.

John and Sanborn agreed to meet later that day at the Washington Square Restaurant. As he left the cabin, John tried to make sense of things. *Why did he hand me a pen that he'd taken from a hotel? Is he proud of that?*

At 9:30 p.m., John arrived at the Washington Square. Sanborn was already there, tucked away in a booth with a woman. John slid into the booth and ordered a drink from the waitress.

Sanborn leaned in and said softly, "Have you had a chance to run the checks on Richard Stratton yet?"

John shook his head. "I don't have his date of birth, but I ran an alphabetical check in our system." He pulled a printout from his pocket and showed it to Sanborn. On the printout was a short list of names—all of them Richard Stratton. John pointed at one of the names. "It's that one there," he said. "This Stratton is listed as residing in Phillips, Maine."

As the conversation continued, John and Sanborn chatted about the airplane that Sanborn had wanted to sell. Sanborn had sold the aircraft to Richard Stratton for $24,000 and pocketed a profit of $11,000. Stratton's nephew would fly the plane.

"I've got friends in Jamaica," said Sanborn. "I travel down there a lot. You know, my friends give me free nights at the motel. And I can get any kind of guns I want down there."

The next several weeks passed without incident. John learned that Sanborn was behind on the rent for his hangar at the airport, and that the airport manager was about to tow Sanborn's plane out of its hangar and park it outside on the ramp. John had several conversations with Linda Prior, who eventually paid the overdue rent.

On March 9, John drove up to Sanborn's house in midafternoon. John got out of his pickup truck and shifted uneasily. Again he had a tape recorder underneath his shirt, taped directly to his skin. The box was at his back, near his belt. The wire ran approximately eighteen inches from the recorder to the microphone taped to John's chest.

As John recalled, "The box was placed on my back in case some girl hugged me, looking for something like a wire. If she did, I'd respond, 'Hey, that's my gun! Don't mess with it.' If someone had asked for me to pull it out, I would simply say, 'No. No one messes with my gun.'"

If Sanborn suspected that he was being recorded, he didn't show it. He and John continued discussing the details of the drug-smuggling operation. John needed more information about the mysterious "big boss," Richard Stratton.

"What role does Stratton have in all this?" John asked.

"He's primarily in the hashish and marijuana business," said Sanborn. "You know that blue van you saw outside my house? Stratton was driving it. We swapped plates. We used Linda's tags."

John nodded. "I'll ignore it when I'm on patrol, of course. But I can't guarantee that another cop won't run the plates."

"We'll be careful," said Sanborn. "We won't do anything unusual with it."

"Still, that's running a big risk."

"It won't be around here much longer," said Sanborn. "Stratton is going to put a false bottom in it. Then he'll use it to run drugs up to Canada."

"That'll work," said John.

At the end of the meeting, Sanborn asked the question that John had been hoping to hear for weeks:

"John, can you meet me at the Washington Square tonight? Because Richard may be around, and you could meet him."

John, of course, agreed. He'd pursued this case for months and had gotten to know Michael Sanborn. Now he was about to meet the man in charge of the entire operation.

Chapter 16

THE MAIN MAN

At 7:30 p.m. on March 9, 1982, John arrived at the Washington Square Restaurant to meet with Michael Sanborn. Half an hour later, Sanborn said:

"My friend Richard just came in. He's at the bar. Do you want to meet him?"

Sanborn retrieved Stratton from the bar and brought him back to the table.

"Richard," said Sanborn, "meet my friend John. He's the cop I told you about."

Sanborn left them alone. John studied Stratton for a moment. Richard Stratton was in his mid-thirties, sharply dressed, friendly but no-nonsense. As he talked, "he looked you straight in the eyes," recalled John, "and spoke in a cold, clear voice. He was very businesslike and appeared to be an upfront, no-bullshit kind of guy."

At first, John was taken aback at Stratton's professionalism and clean-cut demeanor. "He was a different kind of drug dealer than the kind I usually dealt with," John recalled. "I had met plenty of typical scroungy drug dealers, but never someone like this."

"So how do you know Michael?" said Stratton.

"I met him six or seven months ago," said John. "I know what kind of business he's in. I want to be up front with you."

"Well, I'm his boss," said Stratton. "I'm mainly involved in hashish and marijuana. I'm not interested in coke, though—lots of people being killed in Miami; lots of people getting ripped off. Hash and marijuana is in bulk form, so it's harder to rip it off."

"I hear you have a nice place in Texas," said John.

Stratton smiled. "I live up here, in Phillips, on a small farm. But I also have a horse ranch in Texas. It's a thousand acres."

At that point, John directed the conversation toward establishing a relationship.

"How do I know that I can trust you?" said John. "I know Michael, and I trust him. But how can I trust you?"

Stratton smiled. "If you want some references, I'll bring in some of your own people."

"What do you mean?" said John.

"I have some drug enforcement agents whom I'll introduce you to. They'll be my references. They'll flip you a badge [show you their credentials]."

John shook his head. "That's not necessary. I don't need to meet them."

As they talked, Stratton was cordial but protective of his business. John sensed an air of "do not cross me."

Meanwhile, Sanborn returned to the table and sat down.

"Maria called," he said to Stratton. "She wants seventy thousand dollars."

"I'll take care of that later," said Stratton.

John felt the call of nature and excused himself to use the bathroom. As he stood, Sanborn said, "Hey, what's that on your back?" Sanborn pulled a piece of yellow tape from the back of John's shirt.

Shit, thought John. *That's tape from the wire I was wearing earlier today.* Somehow he'd missed it when he removed the recording device. Did Stratton or Sanford know what the tape was for?

This could be the one mistake that flushes the whole case down the drain, thought John. He had to say something, and fast.

"You know how cops are," said John with a chuckle. "They're always playing jokes on each other, like taping signs to your back that say KICK ME."

John waited. *Are they going to buy that explanation?*

Sanborn was laughing. "Do they really do stuff like that?" he said.

He bought it.

"Oh, yeah," said John. "Everyone wants to be a comedian."

On his way back from the restroom, John scanned the dining room and saw two drug enforcement agents from the surveillance team. They were watching him and Stratton.

As John sat down, Sanborn told Stratton, "This is the guy who saved the airplane from being ejected from the hangar at the airport."

John nodded. "The rent wasn't paid, so the airport authorities were going to take the plane out of the hangar."

"Why wasn't the rent paid?" grumbled Stratton. "Next time, Mike, pay the rent, and don't let this happen again. There's no need for it." He turned to John and said, "Can you check out that aircraft, and see if it's hot? My nephew will be flying it out of Sanford in the next few days."

"No problem," said John.

"One other thing," said Stratton, locking eyes with John. "If you turn me or Mike in, there will be ten other people who will take over the business. If you get me arrested, you'll have nothing to gain from it. You have a lot more to gain by working with us."

"I know that," said John.

At the time, John had no idea of the extent to which Stratton had been involved in the drug trade over the years. According to an August 2003 article in *New York* magazine, Stratton was "a middle-class kid from Wellesley, Massachusetts" who dropped out of college to pursue the drug trade:

> He hit the hippie highway, as he puts it, with stops along the way, notably in the Middle East.

There, Stratton befriended some Lebanese Shiites, controllers of the hash trade. ("That was really my area of expertise: being able to get close to those people and get their trust. I tried to give them like a half-million in cash. But a load might cost three or four million.") Soon, he was one of the country's largest importers of high-quality pot and hash.

John Arnold's budding case was about to become a lot more complex.

Chapter 17

GETTING CLOSER

John's next conversation with Sanborn took place at the cabin on March 14. John needed to know if Stratton had bought his story. John looked around for Linda Prior (Sanborn's girlfriend) and another woman he knew. Neither was in the house. Sanborn told him the two women had gone skiing in Vermont. The two men sat down and got comfortable. John had an important question—a question that would determine how his case would proceed:

"How did Richard Stratton like me?"

"He likes you," said Sanborn. "He thought you were a good guy. He felt a lot better about using the Sanford Airport after he talked to you. He's glad you're running security for us at the airport." Sanborn handed John a wad of bills. "He gave me a thousand bucks and told me to split it with you. Here's your half."

John knew better. *Sanborn is lying. I'll bet the entire thousand dollars was meant for me. Drug dealers are thieves, and Sanborn thinks he can get away with cheating his boss a little.*

When he talked about drug running, Sanborn always used the word *business*. This group didn't call themselves smugglers or dealers; they referred to themselves as businesspeople. John was careful to adopt the word as well.

"Okay," said John, "so what am I protecting when I'm doing security at the airport?"

"We're moving fifteen hundred to two thousand pounds at a time—short trips," said Sanborn. "That way, if something happens, we don't lose too much at any one time. Richard can store fifteen hundred pounds at his ranch house up in Phillips."

Still unsure of how the drugs traveled from place to place, John asked for clarification. Sanborn said that Stratton took care of the deals, buying the drugs from outside the United States and making arrangements to transport the product into the country. Once the drugs were in country, Sanborn would stash them somewhere until Stratton gave the go-ahead for the drugs to be transported, often to Canada.

John pressed for more information, careful not to push Sanborn too hard. Sanborn told John that Stratton had stored

1,500 pounds of marijuana at his farm in Phillips at least once before.

"You got anything in the planning stages?" John asked.

"There's a woman, Maria, in Florida. We talked about her a little the other night? Anyway, she's putting together seventy thousand dollars for a shipment. I get ten percent of the load right off the top." Sanborn looked proud of himself. "A pound of marijuana sells for sixteen hundred bucks!"

"Look, you've convinced me," said John. "I like the business. I'll get more out of it than I ever will as a cop. But you need to know that I'm not a drug user. I have a family. So I'll do security for you, but I'll be the security person with the straight head. That way I can have a clear understanding of what is happening around me, for security reasons. Okay?"

Sanborn nodded. "Okay."

"Mike, why is Stratton involved in drug smuggling? He seems pretty well off already."

Sanborn laughed. "How do you think he bought that horse farm in Texas?" He stood up. "Follow me, John. I'll show you around my place." He led John up to the attic, where thirteen marijuana plants grew in pots.

"This is my factory," said Sanborn. He opened a rolltop desk. Inside was some cocaine. He showed John how he separated the coke, on a plate, and made rocks out of it. John had never seen this done before, so he watched the process carefully.

Next stop: the bedroom. Sanborn came out with a one-pound plastic bag of marijuana leaves. He dug inside the bag and handed John a large stem of marijuana plant. It had buds on it.

"It's called sensemilla," Sanborn said. "I've got about a hundred and twenty pounds of it."

"Thanks," said John, "but like I said, I'm not going to use—"

"That's fine," Sanborn interrupted.

I guess he's just trying to show me, as a friend, that he'll give me some drugs even though I won't use them, thought John.

John checked his watch. "I gotta go," he said. "They'll be wondering at the station where I've been."

Later, back at police headquarters, John counted the money that Sanborn had given him. Sanborn had shorted him by twenty dollars.

Chapter 18

MARIA

As JOHN WORKED the case, Capt. Ruel coordinated with the DEA and Agent Wayne Steadman, who wanted to know John's whereabouts anytime he left his house and was dealing with Sanborn or the other members of Stratton's group. "I think it was a shocker to DEA that a small-town cop was infiltrating the Stratton business," recalled John.

Sanborn had taken John under his wing, showing the would-be bad cop the drug business that used hiding locations around Sanford, and the local airport for transportation when needed.

"He began to trust me about everything going on in his business," said John, "except for telling me when a load was arriving at the airport."

John had gotten an eyeful of Sanborn's life: the cabin in the woods, the marijuana plants upstairs, the mini cocaine factory in the rolltop desk, and the fact that 120 pounds of drugs were stashed somewhere in the house.

As far as the investigation was concerned, John was headed in the right direction, toward the ultimate goal: to gather evidence against Richard Stratton, the leader of the operation.

John continued meeting with Sanborn every day or so. Maria, the woman in Florida who was putting together the seventy thousand dollars for the next big buy, appeared in the cabin in mid-March 1982, along with Linda Prior and another woman.

"Stratton used the girls to pick up the money," noted John later. "Before picking up a load, the money had to be paid up front, and Stratton would use the women as runners, or mules."

Sanborn had invited John to visit, but inside the house there were too many people and John felt uncomfortable. When Sanborn handed John a beer, John excused himself to take a leak. He went outside and memorized the plate numbers of the cars parked in the yard.

Later, during another one of John's visits to the cabin, Sanborn finally divulged more details about an upcoming marijuana buy. Sanborn pointed at the blue van and a truck that were parked in his yard, and said that they would use those two vehicles to move the load. Several other men would assist. Sanborn asked John to run checks on the helpers, to see if the police were watching them.

"I think it'll only take us about fifteen minutes to unload the plane," said Sanborn. "There will be thirty to thirty-five bales of marijuana on board."

Unfortunately, John was still unable to get an arrival time out of Sanborn.

The next day, Sanborn filled in more of the story as he and John sat at the kitchen table. The arriving aircraft would have 1,500 pounds of marijuana aboard.

"What'll happen after it arrives?" said John.

"Eventually it'll go out to other people, in hundred-pound shipments."

They discussed what roads to travel when the truck and van left the airport with the drugs. Sanborn said he'd already been down to the airport, around the old tower, and had been scouting out which roads to use.

John, thinking ahead, had brought a three-foot-by-two-foot map of the airport with him. The citywide aerial map showed all of the runways, hangar locations, and roads around the airport. John reviewed the road locations and made suggestions for a getaway route and locations where he could be on the lookout.

On March 20, John met with Sanborn at the Washington Square to discuss more details about the upcoming operation. At one point, Sanborn pulled a small plastic vial from his shirt pocket.

"You don't mind, do you?" he asked John, who shrugged.

Sanborn put the vial to his nose, and snorted.

"I just did a line of coke!" he announced.

After a meal and more discussion, they left the restaurant. As usual, John paid nothing for his meal. Sanborn, as he always did, signaled to their server to "take care of it," and that was that.

Outside, John decided to try another tactic. *I need to find out where the drugs are. Are they already here? Is the shipment on an airplane? Is it at a stash house?*

"Mike, do you have any marijuana that you can front me?"

Sanborn looked confused. "Why? I thought you didn't want to use it for yourself—"

"I don't use it," said John, "but I have friends who do."

Sanborn nodded. "Okay then. Let's go. Let's head up to my house. I'll drive."

John wasn't comfortable with leaving his truck parked at the restaurant. He'd never been alone in a vehicle with Sanborn. But John knew that he had to do something out of the ordinary. He had to ditch the officers and DEA agents who were stationed nearby, ready to jump in and help at any time. John wasn't wearing a wire, and he wasn't carrying a gun. He felt scared and uncomfortable. And when his security backup saw his pickup truck at the restaurant, they'd assume he was still inside.

What John didn't know was that, in a few minutes, he would have a gun pointed at him.

Chapter 19

ALMOST GONE

THE DRIVE TO Sanborn's cabin took fifteen minutes. It was 11:00 p.m when they arrived. The two men got out and headed inside.

This isn't the way things are supposed to happen, thought John. *I'm going to a known drug smuggler's house late at night, I'm not in my own vehicle, and I'm unprepared if something goes south. My backup doesn't know where I am or what I'm doing. I'm completely on my own.*

"I want to show you something," said Sanborn. He headed into the bedroom, and John followed. Inside the bedroom,

Sanborn brought out a Ziploc bag stuffed with buds and stems—marijuana.

"Follow me," said Sanford, bag in hand. He headed downstairs.

As they headed to the first floor, John admired the beautiful open-floor-plan log cabin, with its exposed wooden beams. Sanborn lifted the top of his rolltop desk and took a set of scales out.

"How much do you want?" he asked John.

John needed enough for evidence. "Uh, maybe half a pound?" he said.

Sanborn measured and weighed just under half a pound of marijuana. He bagged it and handed it to John.

"I know you don't use it, like you said," noted Sanborn. "But I know you have a way of getting rid of it. This is just my way of saying that I trust you. Now, let's head back to the bedroom. I want to show you something I got for my birthday."

The two men headed up to the bedroom and sat on opposite sides of the bed. As they continued talking, Sanborn reached underneath the bed and pulled something out. He turned toward John, who froze.

Sanborn was holding an Uzi submachine gun.

John's heart hit the floor. *Oh God*, he thought. *He knows who I really am!*

The gun had what appeared to be a thirty- or thirty-two-round clip in it. Sanborn pointed the barrel at John.

I need to get the gun away from him before he shoots me, thought John.

"I would love to see it!" was the best response that John could muster. Then he grabbed the gun out of Sanborn's hands.

Sanborn laughed. "What do you think? My brother-in-law is from Connecticut, where I used to live. He gave this to me for my birthday!"

What?

"It was a birthday present. I thought you'd like to see it. Pretty cool, huh?"

John checked out the Uzi; he'd never seen one before. It was loaded. He located the magazine release button and pressed it. The magazine dropped out of the weapon and onto the bed. John made sure the chamber was clear. *That's a relief*, he thought to himself. To continue the ruse, John had to act surprised.

"Wow," said John, "it's fully loaded! How many rounds does it hold?"

"Thirty-plus," said Sanborn.

John pointed the Uzi at the wall. "What a weapon!" he said.

He gave the Uzi back to Sanborn. Then he handed Sanborn the magazine.

My first time seeing an Uzi, thought John, *and it's with a drug smuggler.*

Sanborn put away his birthday present and headed downstairs to get a couple of beers. While John waited, he scanned the room. In an ashtray was some drug paraphernalia. There was a bowl and several glass pipes. When Sanborn returned with the beer, he and John sat at a small table to one side of the room. Sanborn had brought some cocaine from downstairs.

"You want to do some?" said Sanborn.

"No," answered John. "I like my beer. Like I told you before, I don't do drugs. I'm just a protector kind of person."

Sanborn nodded. "Well, I'm going to do some freebase and some coke."

He handed John a beer along with a bottle opener. John was relieved that the cap was still on the bottle—there was no telling what Sanborn might have dropped into the bottle had it been open.

"I don't know what freebasing is," said John, "except that Richard Pryor set himself on fire doing it."

Sanborn got excited. "I'll show you."

Sanborn took some coke, put it in a dish, and heated the dish. When the cocaine turned to a brownish-white liquid, he dumped it into a small glass bowl that had a glass straw built into it. Then Sanborn took a cotton swab, placed it in alcohol, and lit the cotton ball on fire. Now he had a small torch. He placed the flame underneath the bowl to heat it.

Once the liquid in the bowl came to a boil, John saw a cloud of smoke inside the bowl that increased to a thick cloud. It reminded him of cigar smoke. Sanborn put the glass straw to his lips and sucked on it. He held the smoke in his lungs, until his face became red and he began to choke on it.

"That's freebasing," explained Sanborn.

He repeated the procedure several more times, becoming very happy and talkative. "I'm beginning to feel good," he said.

Sanborn pulled out a little box with lights on it. "Let me show you this," he said. "It's a voice detection box. It will read your voice. I'm going to find out if you're telling the truth, or if you're lying to me."

Sanborn plugged the machine into the wall but didn't attach anything, such as a wire, to John.

John got a bit nervous, but both men laughed about the little box. To John it appeared to be a voice analysis type of gadget with flashing lights on it. Sanborn told him that if John lied, a red light would flash on the box. If John told the truth, a green light would blink.

"Whatever," said John. "Come on, we're playing a mind game."

We're both laughing, thought John. *I've had a couple of beers, and he's high on coke. This little box is bullshit.*

Sanborn asked his first question. "Are you going to turn me into the police?"

"No," said John. "I *am* the police."

Both men laughed. The green light blinked.

"Okay," said Sanborn. "Next question: Are the DEA enforcement people watching me?"

"No," said John. "They're not watching you. *I* am."

They laughed again, and watched as the light turned green.

Sanborn tried a few more questions without incident. Then John began to turn things around on him. *I need to make him look like the bad guy.*

"Let me ask *you* a question," said John. "Do you really have 1,500 pounds of marijuana, or are you lying to me?"

"I'm telling the truth," said Sanborn.

The green light, of course, came on again.

"Wow, that's a good machine!" said John.

John wasn't sure what the box actually was, but he didn't want to risk exposing himself by answering more questions.

Fortunately, Sanborn was done and unplugged the machine. "You're good, John. No lies," he said.

John had never seen anyone freebase. It felt like a science experiment. *It's amazing to see someone go to such extremes to get high*, he thought. *Maybe while he's high, I can get some more information out of him.* John asked a few questions about the load that was arriving at the Sanford airport.

"Mike, where is the 1,500 pounds of marijuana?"

"Richard has the load all ready," said Sanborn. "He asked me to sit on it."

So the load is already here, thought John. *It must be in a stash house.*

Sanborn told John that the drugs had come from somewhere in the Middle East, maybe Lebanon.

"Bullshit," said John. "I don't believe you." *He's full of crap*, thought John. *He's always playing mind games anyway.*

"That's where he gets it," protested Sanborn. "He has connections."

"No fucking way," said John. "No way somebody brings drugs from overseas, back to our country, and gets it here, to a little town like Sanford, Maine."

As they talked, John learned that the 1,500 pounds of marijuana was actually 1,000 pounds of hash, two or three hundred pounds of marijuana, and some cocaine. Sanborn and another man had driven the pickup truck and the van from New Hampshire to a stash house in Sanford, Maine.

"Were you afraid during the trip?" said John. "I mean, were you afraid that the cops would stop you?"

"Nah," said Sanborn. "I'm not afraid of the cops. Hell, I'm more afraid of being ripped off by other people."

"I'd like to see the stuff," said John. "I've never seen bales that size before."

"The drugs are in boxes, not bales," said Sanborn. "We dropped them off at my brother's house. I'll call him and see if I can get a key, and take you up there." (John would later discover that Sanborn's "brother" wasn't actually his brother at all.) Sanborn got on the phone:

"Hi, Lisa. Let me talk to Matt…. Matt? I have a friend who may want to buy the whole load tonight. Are you going to the club? Can I bring him up? Okay, okay. I understand."

Sanborn hung up and shook his head. "He says no. They're about to move the load over to Richard's place. So, hey, how about tomorrow? I'm going up to Phillips to see Richard anyway. You can come along."

I need to let the department know what's going on, thought John. *But how?*

"Hey, I need to call my wife," said John. "I need to let her know I'm okay and will be home soon, 'cause I've been working late. Can I borrow your phone?"

Sanborn nodded. John rang his boss, Capt. Ruel, at the police station. When the captain answered, John said into the phone, "Hi honey. I just want to let you know that I'm fine, and I'm just working late. I'll be home soon. I had to go to North Berwick to see a friend. But I'll be home soon."

The brief call alerted DEA to John's current location. John hung up and turned back to Sanborn.

"What is Richard going to do with the load, anyway?" said John.

"He wants me to drive it into Canada for him."

"What about using the plane?"

"Richard thought it would be better to drive it to Phillips, and then we can go to Canada from there. We may or may not use the plane."

"Well, if I can help in any way, let me know," said John. "I've never seen that much hash before, and it would be really surprising to see it all."

Next, Sanborn gave John a piece of hashish—about an ounce, which was broken off a quarter-pound block. Sanborn also gave John about a gram of coke that he removed from a blue toolbox. The coke was in the form of a little rock.

"Wow," said John, feigning surprise. "I've never seen this before."

"That coke is about seventy percent pure, John." Sanborn enjoyed playing the role of the teacher.

"Really? I've got some friends who can maybe try it."

Sanborn smiled. "I have something for you that you might need." He reached back into the toolbox and produced a small .32-caliber pistol. He handed John a box of ammunition, followed by the gun.

"You might need this someday," said Sanborn.

At 1:30 a.m., Sanborn drove John back to the Washington Square Restaurant, where John retrieved his pickup truck. Sanborn had put the gifts—hash, rock cocaine, and the pistol—in a paper bag, which he handed to John.

It had been a long night, but John now had plenty of evidence against Sanborn—and Stratton.

Chapter 20

THE ARRESTS

John sat in his truck and watched as Sanborn turned his car around and headed home, passing by police headquarters on the way. When John was satisfied that Sanborn was gone, he drove down the street, past the department, then back into the parking lot. When John walked into police headquarters, he saw DEA Agent Wayne Steadman waiting for him, along with Capt. Ruel.

"I was happy to have gained this new trust," John recalled later, "and to prove to Agent Steadman and Capt. Ruel that

I could handle myself, even if they were upset because they didn't know where I'd been."

John briefed Agent Steadman about what had just happened, and pulled the four items out of his paper sack: marijuana, coke, hashish, and the gun.

Agent Steadman's eyes grew wide. "You've got to be kidding me," he said.

John had located the stash house and had solid proof that the drug-smuggling operation was moving hashish, marijuana, and coke. All of the pieces were coming together quickly—almost *too* quickly. Who would have thought that Sanborn would offer his "new friend" some free drugs and a gun? For the investigation, it was almost a dream come true.

After they congratulated John for the evidence he'd gathered that night, John's supervisors gave him a tongue-lashing.

"Don't pull that again," said Agent Steadman. "You left the restaurant, but you didn't bother to tell us where you were going, how you were getting there, or who you were with."

Capt. Ruel shook his head. "At least you got to a telephone and called. Not that I had fun pretending to be your wife, John."

After eight months of undercover work, it was time to start wrapping things up.

John traveled with Agent Steadman to the federal prosecutor's office in Portland, Maine, to help draw up search and arrest warrants for the principal suspects in the case. John and Agent Steadman arrived at 8:00 a.m. to meet with the federal prosecutor and the judge, who signed the probable cause affidavit and search warrants for all of the locations that law enforcement would visit that day: Sanborn's cabin, Stratton's houses in Maine and Texas, and the stash house in Sanford.

John looked at his watch: it was noon. It was still March 21. He caught himself yawning at one point. He'd been working for twenty-four hours straight.

"As I was leaving Portland with Agent Steadman," John recalled, "the word went out that everything had been signed and search warrants had been issued. All of the places were hit at the same moment so that the suspects didn't have time to warn each other."

Later that day, the task force raided the stash house and the Sanborn cabin. Officers arrested Michael Sanborn and two other suspects, and collected box upon box—John estimated forty or more—of hash, coke, and marijuana. The drugs were loaded into a van and transported back to the evidence room in Sanford. Meanwhile, the vehicles that the suspects had used to haul their drug shipment were towed to a secure area, to be searched later. John noted that the blue van had a false bottom accessible through a panel in the floor, just like Sanborn had said.

So far, everything was proceeding smoothly. But on a sad note, when John arrived at the Sanborn cabin minutes after the raid was over, he saw both of Sanborn's German Shepherds lying dead in the front yard. When the task force had approached the house, the dogs did their job, protecting the cabin, and bit a DEA agent several times. The agent had to shoot both dogs to get them away from him.

John walked into the cabin. Michael Sanborn sat on the

living room couch. A DEA agent stood over him. Sanborn saw John and looked surprised.

"Why did they have to kill my dogs?" said Sanborn.

John had nothing to say. *Heck, I used to play with his dogs*, he thought. *He's just been arrested for drug trafficking, and he's more concerned about his dogs than anything else.*

John read Sanborn his rights as the task force continued its search of the cabin. There were drugs in the rolltop desk, the blue toolbox, and under the bed. There were plastic baggies of marijuana. The Uzi machine gun was still in the bedroom. Everything that John had listed in the search warrant was still in the house.

John headed to the stash house, where the task force had opened one of the boxes of drugs to confirm its contents. The rest of the load—1,000 pounds of hashish, 300 pounds of marijuana, and 8 ounces of coke—was neatly stacked in approximately forty identical boxes piled six feet high and four feet wide. The drugs in the stash house were worth $1.5 million. The shipment was transferred to a walk-in safe at the Sanford police department, to be transferred to a federal storage area later.

At the Sanford airport, the task force searched Sanborn's airplane and his rented hangar.

Meanwhile, in Phillips, Maine, law enforcement arrested Richard Stratton at his farm.

John breathed a sigh of relief. His cover was no longer useful or intact, and he could be himself again. But how would his fellow officers—so used to seeing him as a lush for the past eight months—react?

John had become an outsider in a tiny police department. When they were told that John's behavior had been an act, some of his fellow officers had mixed emotions. "Because it was a small department," John noted, "everyone thought we were close to each other and knew everyone's business.

"The good officers understood why there had to be secrets," John continued, "but a few officers were jealous that I'd been getting so much attention. They were upset that I was unable to trust them with what I was doing, and didn't understand why they couldn't get involved."

Chapter 21

THE GRAND JURY

ON THE MORNING of April 9, 1982—nearly three weeks since the arrests, and eight months after he had launched the investigation of Richard Stratton's drug empire—John Arnold shifted uneasily in his chair. He was sitting inside the U.S. district courthouse in Bangor, Maine, about to testify to a federal grand jury that could indict key players in the drug-running operation. John had spent the morning driving six hours from Sanford to Bangor.

He glanced at a nearby window. Outside, a light snow had begun to fall. He would always remember this day, not only because he was sequestered for the grand jury but also because it was his wife's birthday. He was unable to be with her, unable to go home, and couldn't call her. Peggy had sacrificed a lot for him during the investigation, even when she didn't understand what was happening and he couldn't explain what was going on.

The grand jury's purpose was to hear evidence of probable cause for charges to be filed. As is typical in a grand jury hearing, the defense was not present. Stratton and his group would present their case if they went to trial.

John was a little nervous. Everything he was about to reveal to the grand jury was a result of the investigation he had launched and nurtured. He knew that, in a small way, he was also being judged by the ten members of the grand jury, who sat near him.

As he waited to be questioned, John flipped through his notes and ran through the investigation in his mind at lightning speed. Were there any holes in his police work? *Did I screw up somewhere along the way?* he thought. *Will the grand jury find fault in any of my actions?*

John had testified in court many times during his eleven years as a police officer, but he had never appeared in front of a federal grand jury. He was also anxious to tell his story, finally—even if it was in the secret confines of the grand jury room.

However, he also knew from experience that most of the anxiety would fade away after he answered two or three questions. From that point it would just be John telling a story—a story of the largest land-based hashish smuggling operation ever in the state of Maine at the time.

The lead U.S. attorney on the case, Richard S. Cohen, was

in his fifties and was known for having a high conviction rate. He wore a sharp three-piece pinstripe suit and spoke in a calm, measured voice. As John recalled later, "he was also the kind of guy who was down to earth and did not belittle you."

Next to Cohen were two assistant U.S. attorneys, Margaret McGaughy and William Stokes. Stokes led the questioning.

"Sir," Stokes began, "please state your occupation."

John nodded. "I am a sergeant in the Sanford police department, Sanford, Maine, and have been employed there for approximately eleven years."

Stokes nodded. "Sergeant Arnold, calling your attention to August through September of 1981, did you participate in an investigation?"

"Yes," said John. "I was on surveillance at the time, a surveillance-type situation, on Michael Sanborn and the aircraft at the airport."

The questions kept coming, and John rattled off his answers. Periodically he referred to his notes to refresh his memory. He'd spent too much time and effort on this case to blow it in front of the grand jury.

Then the members of the grand jury had the opportunity to question him.

"Mr. Arnold," asked one juror, "how did Michael Sanborn know that he could trust you?"

"Through our conversations," answered John, "and through the relationship I had built with him."

Another question from the jury: "Were you in uniform or civilian clothes during these meetings with Mr. Sanborn?"

"I was in civilian clothes at all of the meetings, except on one occasion when I was in uniform, in a police cruiser. On that occasion, Mr. Sanborn met up with me just to say hi."

A juror wanted details of John's visit to Sanborn's cabin on the day that Sanborn produced drugs and a gun.

"Did Mr. Sanborn get suspicious when you asked him for samples of the drugs?"

"At the time," answered John, "I thought that Mr. Sanborn was high enough, and that he looked to me as a friend whom he had taken under his wing. He was totally high."

One juror asked about the wire that John had worn during his conversations with Sanborn. "Wouldn't it have been curtains for you if Mr. Sanborn had detected that you were wearing a wire?"

John nodded. "I would have to do some fast talking, yes."

"I thought it would have been the end," said the juror.

"Quite possibly," said John. "On one occasion, Mr. Sanborn had a machine that he put me on. It's called a 'voice stress analyzer.' However, it didn't affect my investigation."

The jury's questions turned to the events that occurred at the airport.

"Can you confirm that you were first engaged to guard the plane for Mr. Sanborn?"

"Yes," said John. "I was responsible for watching for security of the airport and his people."

Another juror raised her hand. "Mr. Arnold," she said, "On the trip to Canada, why did Mr. Sanborn get mad at the pilot?"

"The pilot wouldn't land in Canada because the wings were iced up."

"Mr. Arnold, what happened to the Beechcraft, and did Mr. Sanborn ever purchase a second airplane?"

John nodded. "Mr. Sanborn told me he sold the Beechcraft to Richard Stratton. After that, Mr. Sanborn planned to purchase an Aero Commander twin-engine aircraft. However, I don't know if Mr. Sanborn ever did acquire the Aero Commander."

Testimony went on all day. When it was over in the late afternoon, the snowstorm had become a blizzard—an unexpected one, so late in the winter. As John left the courthouse, he had to trudge through a foot of snow on the ground. He realized that he wouldn't be able to get home. All of the roads were closed.

John stayed the night in a hotel. He was finally able to call his wife and make sure that she and the kids were safe.

"My brothers will come over to shovel and plow us out," Peggy told him.

Several days later, the roads were clear enough for John to drive home. Meanwhile, his brother-in-law had to rescue Peggy from inside the house. The snowfall in Sanford was stacked so high that it had covered the doors and windows.

UNITED STATES MARSHALS SERVICE

WANTED
BY U.S. MARSHALS

NOTICE TO ARRESTING AGENCY: BEFORE ARREST, VALIDATE WARRANT THROUGH NATIONAL CRIME INFORMATION CENTER (NCIC).

UNITED STATES MARSHALS SERVICE NCIC ENTRY NUMBER: (NIC/____W2875480974____).

NAME: Stratton, Richard L.

AKA(S): Richard Lowell,Richard Lowe,R.McIlveen

DESCRIPTION:
SEX   Male
RACE   White
PLACE OF BIRTH Boston Mass
DATE(S) OF BIRTH 01 13 46
HEIGHT   6 ft
WEIGHT   200
EYES   Blue
HAIR   Brown
SKINTONE   Med.
SCARS, MARKS, TATOOS 12 in scarRt.Hip
SOCIAL SECURITY NUMBER(S) 013 34 4048
NCIC FINGERPRINT CLASSIFICATION:

ADDRESS AND LOCALE: Res.Phillips Maine
                      Has Associates in Hawaii,Texas,California,

WANTED FOR: Failure to Appear T18 USC 3150
   WARRANT ISSUED: July 23,1982
   WARRANT NUMBER: 8236 0723 0033A
DATE WARRANT ISSUED: July 23,1982

MISCELLANEOUS INFORMATION: FBI # 481641 R6   Epic#I 82-1524--Has Pilots License
                            using a Cherokee 6 #N1445X

VEHICLE/TAG INFORMATION:

IF ARRESTED OR WHEREABOUTS KNOWN, NOTIFY THE LOCAL UNITED STATES MARSHALS OFFICE,
   (TELEPHONE ____207 780 3355____). FTS 833-3355
IF NO ANSWER, CALL UNITED STATES MARSHALS SERVICE COMMUNICATIONS CENTER IN WASHINGTON, D.C.
   TELEPHONE ____703 285 1100____ . NLETS ACCESS CODE IS DCUSMO0OD.
        (24 Hour telephone contact)

Chapter 22

STRATTON ON TRIAL

THE GRAND JURY indicted fifteen people who had been part of the drug-running operation, including Richard Stratton. All of them were arrested and charged with felonies in federal court.

Stratton made bail but failed to show at his hearing. On July 23, 1982, the U.S. Marshals Service issued a fugitive warrant for his arrest. Stratton was found in Los Angeles, where he was finally arrested in August. He was sent back to Maine.

Meanwhile, Michael Sanborn had to answer for the traffic accident he had caused in January. He pled guilty and was convicted of manslaughter for killing the other driver. He went to prison while the Stratton case was pending trial.

Sanborn's former boss, Richard Stratton, was sitting in federal prison. Since he was a fugitive and had skipped his first hearing, he had no bail set and had to remain in prison until the trial, which was scheduled to begin in September 1982 in Portland, Maine.

Meanwhile, three of Stratton's underlings in Texas were arrested. They agreed to a plea bargain.

In March 1983—a year after Stratton's arrest—John Arnold prepared to testify at the federal trial. U.S. Attorney Cohen was the prosecutor. Michael Sanborn agreed to testify against his old boss. In exchange, he pled guilty to conspiracy and would serve a five-year federal sentence concurrently with the time he was already serving on his vehicular manslaughter charge.

During the trial, Stratton fired his attorneys and decided to represent himself. Tall, thin, and well dressed, Stratton "looked like a guy with all the right questions and answers," recalled John. "He was very bold and very smart, confident and sure of himself."

As the trial continued, Stratton, who wasn't trained as a lawyer, periodically interrupted the proceedings. "The judge had to quiet him down more than once," John recalled.

Throughout the three-week trial, Richard Stratton maintained that he was actually a writer and not a well-connected drug smuggler. According to the Associated Press, "the defense portrayed Stratton as an aspiring writer who got caught up in the shadowy world of big-time drug dealing, but never crossed the line from observer to participant."

Stratton's interest in writing was not new: he had been writing about the drug trade since the 1970s. He was originally a caretaker of the farm in Phillips, Maine, and eventually became co-owner with the well-known novelist Norman Mailer, who testified in Stratton's defense during the trial.

Michael Sanborn testified for four days, verifying that Stratton had been his boss in the drug-smuggling operation.

In the end, the jury didn't buy Stratton's "writer's defense" and found him guilty of conspiracy to smuggle marijuana and hashish. Stratton was sentenced to fifteen years in federal prison.

In the Region

6/7/83

C. Scott Hoar photo

Top cop

Sanford Sgt. John A. Arnold displays the plaque he received from the New England Narcotics Enforcement Officers Association last week as the six-state region's outstanding officer of the year. He was cited for his work in late 1981 and early 1982 which concluded with the breakup of an international drug smuggling and distribution ring in Maine.

From the *York County Journal Tribune.*

Chapter 23

CASE CLOSED

AND WHAT HAPPENED to Michael Sanborn, the man who worked for Richard Stratton, and who showed undercover cop John Arnold how Stratton's drug-running operation worked?

By 1985 the courts had finished with the Stratton trial, and Sanborn was out of jail after serving thirty months of his five-year prison sentence. Sanborn returned to Sanford, got a job in a local factory, and lived a quiet life.

Then, in the fall of that year, the Maine State Police investigated an early-morning murder:

Sanborn was found shot to death in Sanford, Maine, on September 16, 1985 at 0725 hours. The murder was determined to be execution style. The body was located lying next to his vehicle in a parking lot at Providence Automation Company in the Adams Industrial Park in Sanford, Maine.

Sanborn had a drug history and had been doing maintenance work at the factory. Suspects have been interviewed.

The police were unable to close the case, and to this day Sanborn's murder remains unsolved. The information above appears on the website of the Maine State Police as a cold case.

Meanwhile, another participant in the drug-smuggling operation was also murdered.

The DEA called John, and Wayne Steadman and another agent visited John in Sanford. They told John to watch his back.

As John recalled: "Of course, the two murders *could* have been connected, but they weren't sure. But because of the drug investigation—because of the high-class clientele of Richard Stratton and Stratton's drug connection in Canada, whom I knew nothing about—they put me on notice to be aware that my name had been mentioned at one point by an informant. They even said I was on a hit list. It gave me the impression to be really careful."

Meanwhile, Stratton served eight years in prison. He appealed his sentence, was released on parole, and went on to a successful second career as a novelist and producer for television and film.

In late 2014, Stratton began releasing chapters from *Smuggler's Blues*, the first book of his three-volume autobiography. In a November 2014 interview, website *The Reading Room* asked Stratton if he'd left out any details. "No, I put it all in," he replied, "including the regrets, the shame I feel for the way I sometimes acted—so full of hubris. And for the people my actions hurt—some deep regrets."

Looking back on the biggest case of his career, John Arnold recalled the seat-of-the-pants nature of the case. "The investigation wasn't put together with any great thought," he said. "It was put together day by day, week by week, and by going with the flow."

Throughout the investigation, John was unaware of just how far Richard Stratton's network stretched. "There were little things the higher government agencies never told me," said John, "and they probably had their reasons, I'm sure. At the time I didn't know that this guy was a major player whom they'd been after for years."

There were also certain police procedures that wouldn't be allowed if the investigation took place today, "like going into somebody's house alone and not having a wire, or maybe not carrying a gun on a particular day to meet these guys," said John. "Those things you just can't do today, but back in my day we did things that we had no other way of doing because of a lack of equipment or a lack of people to surveil you."

Despite the danger involved, John felt relatively comfortable as he moved through the investigation. Law enforcement personnel, noted John, develop a "sixth sense" on the job. "I think we learn to read people," he explained. "We read them in such a way that we can figure things out before they do what they're going to do."

When the Stratton case was over, John continued working for the Sanford PD for several more years. He then moved his family from Maine to Arkansas, where his mother was ill with cancer. He applied for several local law enforcement positions but was told that he was overqualified. After spending four years as a regional manager for a security company, John became tired of the drudgery of hiring and firing people. He considered reapplying for a law enforcement job, but after years of working nights and weekends for a police department, he wanted something that allowed him to spend more time with his wife and children.

And so, in 1993, the experienced police officer took a new job with a small-town police department, this time in Arkansas. His title: animal control officer.

"As it turns out," John explained, "Arkansas is a great place to raise a family."

About the Authors

DARRYL J. KIMBALL, a retired sergeant and helicopter pilot with the San Diego Sheriff's Department, came to California from his hometown of Oktaha, Oklahoma. After 15 years on the patrol beat, he joined the department's air unit, ASTREA (Aerial Support to Regional Enforcement Agencies), in 2005. Darryl runs the popular blog policehelicopterpilot.com. His book *Catch the Sky: The Adventures and Misadventures of a Police Helicopter Pilot*, which he cowrote with Allan Duffin, was inspired by his blog and life story. He, his wife Angela, and their two children live in San Diego.

ALLAN T. DUFFIN is a writer/producer based in Austin, Texas. A veteran of the U.S. Air Force, he is the co-author, with Darryl Kimball, of *Catch the Sky: The Adventures and Misadventures of a Police Helicopter Pilot*; author of *History in Blue: 160 Years of Women Police, Sheriffs, Detectives, and State Troopers*; and co-author of *The "12 O'Clock High" Logbook: The Unofficial History of the Novel, Motion Picture, and TV Series*. His Web site is www.aduffin.com.